The Art & Science of Coaching Series

S0-CFU-716

ALL-PURPOSE OFFENSES
FOR MEN'S AND WOMEN'S BASKETBALL

Harry L. "Mike" Harkins
Jerry Krause

COACHES CHOICE

©1997 Coaches Choice Books. All rights reserved. Printed in the United States.

No part of this book may be reproduced, stored in a retrieval system, or transmitted, in any form or by any means, electronic, mechanical, photocopying, recording, or otherwise, without the prior permission of Sagamore Publishing, Inc.

ISBN: 1-57167-140-4
Library of Congress Catalog Card Number: 97-67167

Book Layout: Michelle A. Summers
Cover Design: Deborah M. Bellaire
Cover Photos: Left—Courtesy of Duke University
              Right—Courtesy of University of Tennessee
Diagrams: Deborah M. Bellaire

Coaches Choice Books is an imprint of: Sagamore Publishing, Inc.
                                                P.O. Box 647
                                                Champaign, IL 61824-0647
                                                (800) 327-5557
                                                (217) 359-5940
                                                Fax: (217) 359-5975
                                                Web Site: http//www.sagamorepub.com

DEDICATION

This book is dedicated to my wife, Grace, who, along with being the love of my life, has been a working partner in the books I have written. Without her meticulous efforts on the diagrams and hours spent typing, they might never have been completed.

—H. L. H.

This book is dedicated to all those who have been given unique talents to play the great game of basketball. May they acknowledge that gift by always giving something back to the game. May this basketball coaching series be a gift to basketball from the authors who have received so much from the sport.

—J. K

ACKNOWLEDGMENTS

Grateful appreciation is expressed to the sources of my basketball knowledge, including: Russ Estey and Mike Krino, my high school coaches; Russ Beichly and Red Cochrahe, my college coaches; Buck Hyser, who gave me my first coaching job; and the players who have played on my teams.

A final note of thanks goes to my children—Mike and his wife, Diane; Patti and her husband, Ric; and Jim and his wife, Jeanne—and my number one fans, my grandchildren, Shellee, Jamee, Mike, Shawn, and Walker.

A special acknowledgment goes to Jerry Krause for his diligent efforts in helping me complete this book.

CONTENTS

PREFACE

These basketball coaching books for men and women coaches are a complete, comprehensive series of books designed to cover all prominent offensive and defensive techniques and strategies used in basketball, i.e., the X's and O's of the sport.

All coaches are reminded that all individual and team basketball is dependent upon individual fundamental skills. You need to ensure that your players are fundamentally sound in order to be able to execute offenses and defenses. Thus, fundamentals are always needed *before* the X's and O's of basketball.

Coaches at all levels will be able to utilize this complete series of men and women's books either as a complete package or as an integrated supplement to presently used offenses and defenses. There is something for every coach, from the novice to the most experienced basketball wizard. It is our intent to meet the needs of all coaches at all levels of play—develop and enjoy your special approach to the X's and O's of basketball.

INTRODUCTION

How All-Purpose Offenses Will Help Your Team

The techniques contained within this book are some of the most successful offensive team techniques currently being utilized in the game of basketball. These techniques are representative of the changes that have been made since the advent of the shot clock and the three-point play.

The Primary Plan

The first eight chapters contain offenses that can be used as part of a team's primary offensive plan. These offenses include quick-hitting entries like the stack, the UCLA slash play, and dribble entry plays. Offenses with multi-option continuities are also included, so that teams can develop the versatility needed to obtain a quick shot when they are trailing in the game. This versatility will also allow an offense to work the defense and kill the clock in search of a high-percentage shot when protecting a precarious lead.

Special Situations

Chapters nine and ten are designed to help an offense during a game's closing minutes. Each chapter provides an offense with ultra-quick shot options that can be used when a team is playing "catch-up" and time is of the essence. For the times when a team is protecting a close lead and faces many critical possessions, an out-and-out control game is offered to help an offense kill the clock and resort to the previously mentioned ultra-quick shot options to obtain a high-percentage shot. High-percentage shots are made possible by the fact that the control game and the ultra-quick offense are run from the same offensive set. Up-tempo teams may also use the ultra-quick offense as a primary offense.

The eight primary offenses are based on the fundamentals utilized by a player-to-player offense. A well-planned modern offense should:

1. Have potential for the three-point play in order to open up the inside game.
2. Have an inside threat that facilitates its three-point options. In other words, the offense should be built from the inside out.
3. Relieve ballside pressure with dribble entries and backdoor plays.
4. Have an offensive rebounding plan without sacrificing defensive balance.
5. Contain both quick-shot and clock-killing elements.
6. Be adaptable to use against combination, changing, and disguised zone defenses.
7. Be adaptable to double-teaming pressure.
8. Utilize the talent available to the team.
9. Encourage individual initiative with optional play variations, meaning players should be allowed to use their individual strengths within the team system of play.
10. Attack the defense in a variety of ways.

The eight offenses are subdivided as follows:

1. Basic Play — the heart of the offense.
2. Play Variation — an optional phase.
3. Pressure Reliever — methods of relieving ballside pressure.
4. Secondary Plays — extra plays that may be added when and if needed.
5. Zone Potential — How the basic player-to-player offense may be adapted to be run against zone defenses.

Explaining all the X and O material found in purpose offenses will help coaches clarify their offensive philosophies and evaluate their present plans from offensive and defensive standpoints. We are positive that coaches will find several ideas to utilize as key ingredients in their future offensive plans.

—Mike Harkins and Jerry Krause

Player #1 passes to #2

Player #1 dribbles the ball

Player #4 passes to Player #2 and then screens for Player #3 cutting

Right arm of Defender #3
Back of Defender #3
Left arm of Defender #3

OFFENSE

① Player #1 with the ball

② Player #2 with the ball

③ Player #3 with the ball

④ Player #4 with the ball

⑤ Player #5 with the ball

DEFENSE

X_1 Defender guarding Player #1

X_2 Defender guarding Player #2

X_3 Defender guarding Player #3

X_4 Defender guarding Player #4

X_5 Defender guarding Player #5

CHAPTER 1

The Passing Game Plus

One of the most effective ways to utilize the passing game is to coordinate it with other patterns. This chapter shows how it may be used, along with the shuffle, the pivot pull-out pattern, the double screen play, or the reverse action pattern.

The Mixer Passing Game

The passing game used in this chapter is a very simple one. We call it "the mixer." It is run from a 1-2-2 set and initiated from a double stack on the "block" area of the free throw lane. As (1) brings the ball up to the head of the key, the two underneath stackers ((2) and (3)) pop out of the downscreens of their respective top players ((4) and (5)). They will end up in the formation seen in Diagram 1-1. (1) passes to either wing, and two simple rules are followed: (A) a point-to-wing pass calls for screening away, and (B) a wing-to-point pass keys a double downscreen.

Basic Pattern

Screen Away
When (1) passes to (2) in Diagram 1-1, this point-to-wing pass tells (1) to screen away for (3), who cuts to the point. It also keys (4) to screen away for (5), who cuts to the ballside post area. Both (3) and (5) are scoring options and they should be prepared to catch the ball in an all-purpose position. This is best accomplished by using a jump stop in a low stance. The players should be taught to say to themselves, "ball in the air, feet in the air," in order to *catch* all passes with their feet in the air and *make* all passes with their feet on the floor. When practiced enough, this prevents the players from catching the ball in a stride stop and then traveling by pivoting on their front foot to face the basket.

Note also that perimeter players need to get open from the defender to receive a pass. This can be done with a V-cut or an L-cut as shown in Diagram 1-1. The rule is to go to the basket or the defender before you cut quickly to get open, i.e., get close to get open.

Screen Away
Diagram 1-1

Screen Down

If (2) passes to (5) in the post, (5) usually shoots the ball. When (2) passes to (3), a shot may be taken, but it is better to continue to move the defense. This is done by having (2) and (1) downscreen for (4) and (5), who pop to their respective wings. See Diagram 1-2.

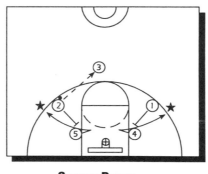

Screen Down
Diagram 1-2

The mixer process is repeated until a high-percentage shot develops.

This motion has had a recent revival of popularity, but it is now being combined and/or alternated with other types of motion. This provides the variety that is needed and, in turn, makes it harder to defend.

The Mixer Plus the Shuffle

For this offense, the mixer is alternated with a lob shuffle motion. The mixer portion is run with its screen down and screen away rules. It is keyed as before with the two inside stackers popping to the wings. See Diagram 1-3. The shuffle phase is keyed when the two top stackers ((4) and (5)) pop to the wings. See Diagram 1-4.

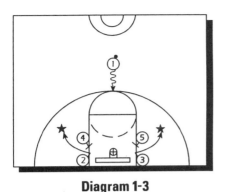

Diagram 1-3 | Diagram 1-4

Basic Pattern

The Shuffle Phase

The shuffle portion of this offense begins when the big players ((4) and (5)) at the top of the stacks pop to the wing positions at the free throw line extended. (1) passes to one of them (as to (4) in Diagram 1-5), and screens opposite for the other wing player (5). However, (2), in the ballside post, does not screen away. (2) moves to a position half-way to the ballside corner (short corner) and (3) cuts to the ballside high post.

This alignment puts two big (and often awkward) defenders (X4 and X5) on the perimeter, which is usually out of their element. (4) reverses the ball to (1) by way of (5) at the point, and makes a shuffle cut off (3) to the ballside low post area. This cut leads to a lot of baskets because X4 is not used to getting through perimeter screens and X3 probably will not "hedge out" to help defend the cutter (4). See Diagram 1-6.

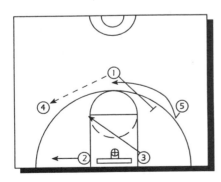

Wing to Big Entry
Diagram 1-5

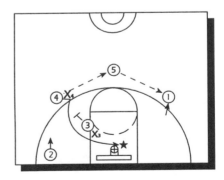

Shuffle Cut
Diagram 1-6

(2) replaces (4) at the wing, as (3) moves up to set a screen that allows (5) to cut to the offside lay-up area for a possible lob pass. See Diagram 1-7. Again, X5 is not well versed in perimeter defense and (5) might be wide open.

These are two excellent scoring options and they also return the team to its basic set with the big players ((4) and (5)) in the posts and the smaller players ((I), (2), and (3)) on the perimeter. See Diagram 1-8.

From there, they can resume the mixer motion.

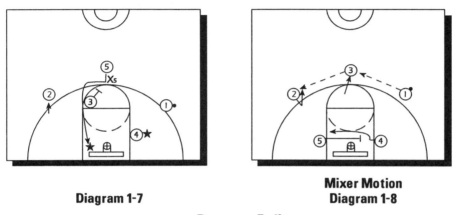

Diagram 1-7

Mixer Motion
Diagram 1-8

Pressure Reliever

The Backdoor Play

The shuffle phase was keyed when big players (4) and (5) cut to their respective wings from the initial stack set. This put two big defenders into areas usually covered by smaller, quicker players. To further take advantage of this alignment, a backdoor play is included. As (4) and (5) reach their wing areas, the two offensive players now in the post positions break up and one of them ((2) in Diagram 1-9) receives a bounce pass from (1). At that time, the defenders on (4) and (5) are usually attempting to deny the point-to-wing pass in a less than functional defensive stance. The pass to (2) tells (4) to backdoor X4 and very often leads to an easy lay-up shot. (3) adds a second option by wheeling on the defender and looking for a pass from (2) or from (4) along the baseline, i.e., provide a "baseline release" for all the baseline ball penetration from the opposite side. This happens if X3 helps X4 on the backdoor move. The best pass for (2) to use to the backdoor cutter (5) is almost always a two-hand bounce pass, i.e., catch the ball with feet in the air at the elbow and make the two-hand pass with your back to the basket.

If no one is open, (2) returns the ball to (1) then (2) and (3) cross to use (4) and (5)'s downscreens to pop to the wings. This puts the team back into its original set, and the mixer may be run. See Diagram 1-10.

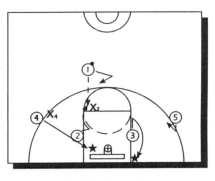

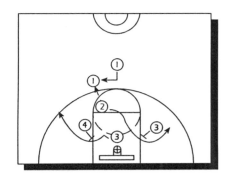

Shuffle Backdoor
Diagram 1-9

Diagram 1-10

This idea of coordinating the passing game with other types of motion probably received its major impetus from Dean Smith's TarHeels, and is now being widely used. Following are some other offensive motions that combine well with the mixer.

The Mixer Plus the Post Pullout Motion

The same keys that were used to differentiate between the mixer and the shuffle are used again for this offense. When the small inside players pop out of the stack, it calls for the mixer (see Diagram 1-11). The post pullout motion is keyed when the big players cut to the wings. See Diagram 1-12.

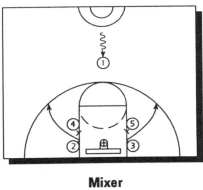

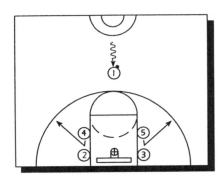

Mixer
Diagram 1-11

Shuffle
Diagram 1-12

The Post Pullout Motion

Basic Pattern
The top stackers pop out, and (1) passes to (4), and screens away for (5) at the opposite wing position. However, this time, the onside post (2) has cleared the post area and looped around the offside post (3). See Diagram 1-13.

This post pullout maneuver allows (5) to use (1)'s screen and cut all the way to the basket on the ballside. When this play is used after the mixer has been run, it often results in an easy lay-up shot. See Diagram 1-14.

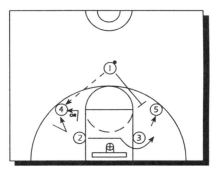

**Post Pullout
Diagram 1-13**

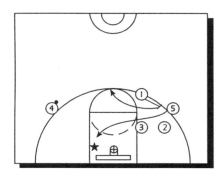

Diagram 1-14

If the pass is not made to (5), (4) passes to (1), who makes a replacement cut back to the point, and the pattern is repeated. See Diagrams 1-15 and 1-16.

At this juncture, the team has returned to its original set with (4) and (5) in the post positions.

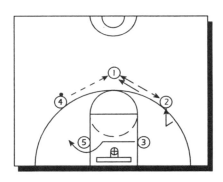

**Post Pullout
Diagram 1-15**

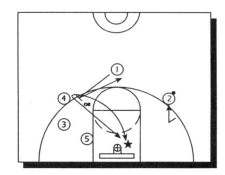

Diagram 1-16

Post Pullout Variations

Three simple pattern variations that may be used with the post pullout motion are the switch, the loop, and the low cut. They are of special value because they may be inserted spontaneously by the players without interrupting the basic pattern.

I. The Switch

This time when (1) passes to a wing (as to (4) in Diagram 1-17) and screens away for the other wing (5), and calls out "switch!" This call tells (5) to cut to the point. (1) then back pivots or executes a rear turn (here using the right foot as a pivot), and rolls to the ballside lay-up area. See Diagram 1-18.

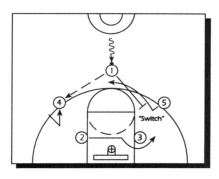

Post Pullout Switch
Diagram 1-17

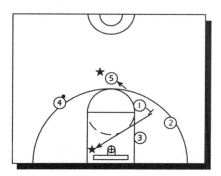

Rear Turn Diagonal Cut
Diagram 1-18

If (1) is not open, (4) passes to (5) and the post pullout motion continues. See Diagram 1-19.

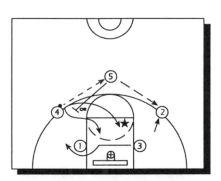

Post Pullout
Diagram 1-19

II. The Flash Variation

(1) again passes to (4) and screens away for (5), who cuts to the area that was cleared by (2). See Diagram 1-20.

This time, however, (1) does not make a replacement cut to point. Instead, the player (1) continues on for (2)'s defender and nails X2 with a definite screen. (2) uses (1)'s screen to flash to the point and receive the ball from (4), for an unmolested jump shot. This shot can be a three pointer if desired. See Diagram 1-21.

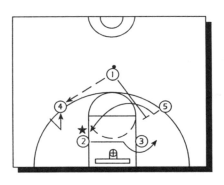

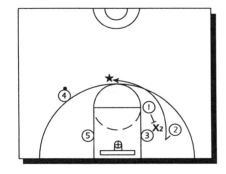

Diagram 1-20

Post Pullout Loop
Diagram 1-21

If (1) is not open, the motion is repeated.

(1)'s screen can be a very active head-hunting screen.

III. The Low Cut

The third variation for the post pullout play is the option for (5) to cut low off post (2), who vacated the ballside post. See Diagram 1-22.

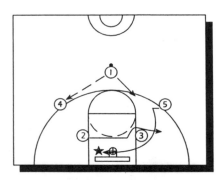

Post Low Cut Pullout
Diagram 1-22

If (5) is not open, (1) makes a replacement cut at the point, and the next option may be run. See Diagrams 1-23 and 1-24.

These variations may be keyed spontaneously by the players as the pattern is in motion. The post pullout concept works very well in conjunction with the mixer. It gives the offense depth by making it difficult to predict and prepare to defend.

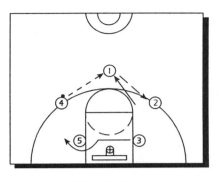

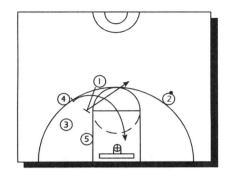

Post Pullout
Diagram 1-23

Diagram 1-24

The Mixer Plus the Double Downscreen Play

Basic Pattern

This offense consists of the mixer and the double downscreen play being run interchangeably. Diagrams 1-25 and 1-26 show the mixer in progress with passes from point-to-wing keying a screen away, and passes from the wing to point calling for double downscreens.

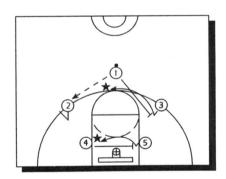

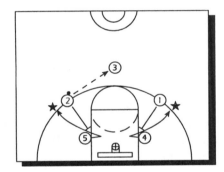

Screen Away
Diagram 1-25

Screen Down
Diagram 1-26

The double downscreen play is *called by a post* (as by (2) in Diagram 1-27) after the screen away phase. When (3) passes to (5), he or she screens away. Onside post (2) calls the play by screening away for (1), and then popping to the mid-high post area to "catch and face" the basket. (5) attempts to pass to (2). If X1 is fronting (1), (2) may be able to get the ball to (1) for a power lay-up shot. See Diagram 1-27. When (4) sees (2) in the high post, he or she doubles back to screen for (3). This gives (2) room to work. See Diagram 1-28.

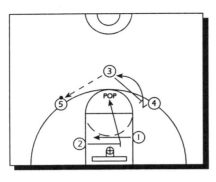

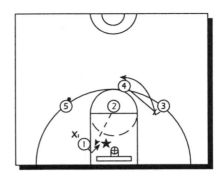

Post Pop
Diagram 1-27

Diagram 1-28

If (5) cannot get the ball to (2), (5) passes to (3), who reverses it to (4). See Diagram 1-29.

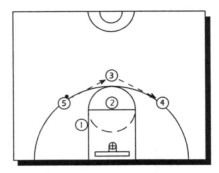

Diagram 1-29

The double downscreen is then executed with (3) and (2) coming down together to screen for (1). (5) uses this moving double screen by rubbing off defender to the ballside low post. See Diagram 1-30.

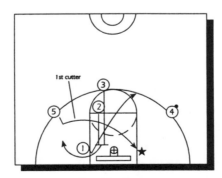

Double Down
Diagram 1-30

If (5) is not open, (4) passes to (1) and the double stack is repeated with (4) screening down for (5) and (3) looping around (2). (1) can then pass to a wing as to (3) in Diagram 1-31 and the mixer is restarted. See Diagram 1-32.

The double-down phase is keyed again whenever the ballside post screens away and then pops to the high mid-post area.

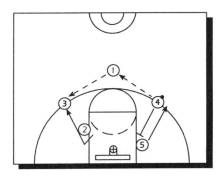

Diagram 1-31

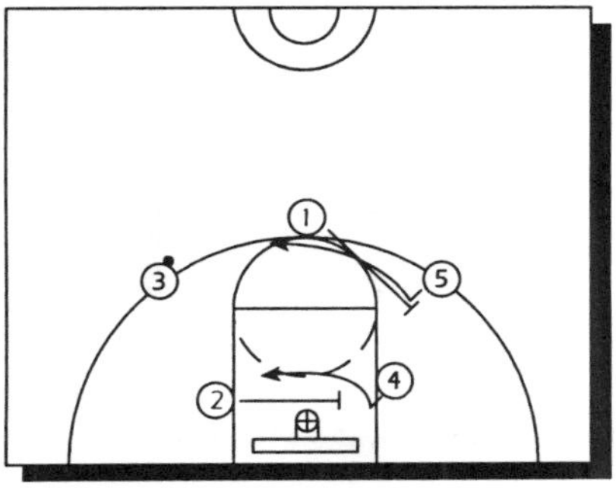

Screen Away
Diagram 1-32

The Mixer with a Reverse Action Phase

Basic Pattern
In Diagram 1-33, (1) starts the mixer by passing to a wing ((2)) and screening for the offside wing (3), who cuts to the point. The ballside post (4) keys/calls the reverse action phase by cutting to the ballside corner instead of screening away for (5). (5) still comes to the ballside mid-post area.

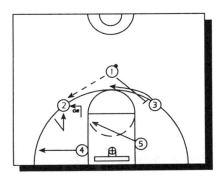

Ballside Post to Corner
Diagram 1-33

(2) then passes to (3), who reverses the ball to (1). (2) and (4) make their scissors-type reverse action cuts. (3) must delay the cut down and inside (5) until (2) gets by. See Diagrams 1-34 and 1-35. If (2) is not open, (1) passes to (4) and a double stack is formed with (1) screening down for (2), and (3) looping around (5)'s downscreen. See Diagram 1-34.

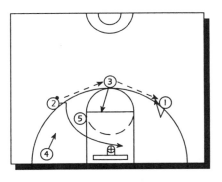

Reverse Action
Diagram 1-34

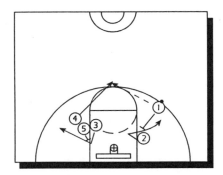

Diagram 1-35

(4) may then pass to either wing and restart the mixer.

These four offenses are examples of how the passing game can be improved by alternating, or combining it with other types of motion. This gives it the added depth needed to make it difficult to scout, plan for, and defend against.

Zone Potential

One of the basic passing game maneuvers is the quick cut. It consists of a pass followed by a cut to the basket much like the old give-and go play. When this is done after many passing game-type passes and screen away moves, it is very effective. It can also serve as the basis of a passing game zone offense.

Quick Cut to an Overload

Diagram I -36 shows point (1) of a 1-2-2 set pass to wing (2) and make a quick cut down the middle and to the ballside corner. (4) helps (1) get open by screening the zone and impeding its slides to cover (1). (3) replaces (1) at the point.

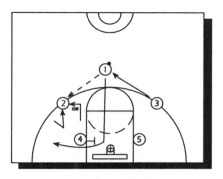

Quick Ballside Cut
Diagram 1-36

This overload is maintained (see Diagram 1-37) until the middle perimeter player decides to balance the offense by passing to (3) and making a quick cut to the opposite wing. See Diagram 1-38. (1) then replaces (2) at the wing.

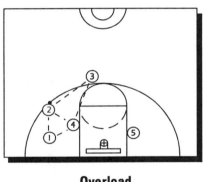

Overload
Diagram 1-37

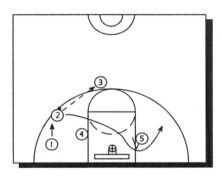

Balance
Diagram 1-38

Quick Cut to the Overshift

This time, when (1) makes the quick cut down the middle after passing to a wing (as to (2) in Diagram 1-39), (1) swings around (5). (5) screens the zone and the ball quickly is reversed to (4) via (3) at the point.

If (1) is not open, the ball is passed around the perimeter until (3), the new middle player decides to cut through. Player (3) can then call an overload or an overshift play by the direction of the cut.

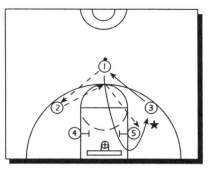

Quick Offside Overshift Cut
Diagram 1-39

The Triangle Play

The triangle play is called by the middle player when the offense is balanced. In Diagram 1-40, (1) passes to (2) and moves away as if to screen for (3). (3) can then do one of two things: (A) (3) can simply replace (1) at the point. When this happens, the players continue to pass the ball on the perimeter.

Or (B) (3) can cut to the middle of the zone. Then if (2) can get the ball to (3), (3) can shoot or catch and face and drop it inside to (4) or (5). When (1) sees (3) cut to the middle, (1) moves out to three-point range. See Diagram 1-41.

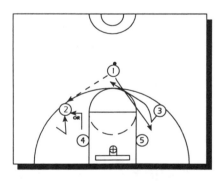

Diagram 1-40

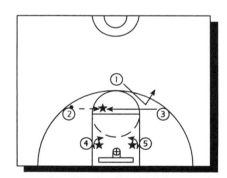

Middle Triangle Cut
Diagram 1-41

If (2) cannot get the ball inside, (3) clears down the lane to an overload (see Diagram 1-42) or overshift (see Diagram 1-43) position, and (1) replaces at the point.

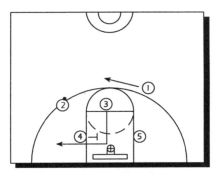

Triangle to Overload
Diagram 1-42

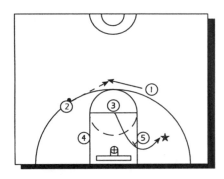

Diagram 1-43

From there, any of the three plays (overload, overshift, or triangle) may be run.

This zone offense is based on passing game principles. It overloads, overshifts, screens, and tests the middle of the zone. It is very easy to teach to passing game teams.

CHAPTER 2

The Stacked UCLA Shuffle

This motion starts in a double stack, follows with the UCLA slash play, and concludes with a shuffle pattern. That combination of top offensive maneuvers should lead to many high-percentage shot opportunities. The inclusion of quick-shot options (stack and UCLA slash cut) and the clock-killing shuffle will help a team meet the time constraints of "shot clock" basketball.

The stacked UCLA shuffle is a continuity that interchanges all five players. This makes it best suited for teams that lack a dominant big player.

The Basic Pattern

Diagram 2-1 shows the double stack open up as (1) reaches the head of the key. (1) passes to wing (2) and slashes off (4) to the ballside low post. (4) must cut to the high post after the popout screen for (2) and before (1) makes the cut to avoid a foul being called.

(4) then steps out to receive a pass from (2), who screens down for (1). (1)'s rule is to "put your head under the basket" before your pop cut using the down screen to cut to the wing (ala UCLA). See Diagram 2-2.

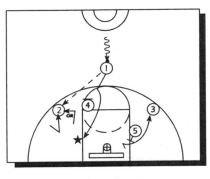

UCLA Slash
Diagram 2-1

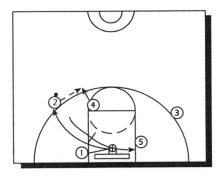

Pop Cut
Diagram 2-2

However, (2), after screening, does not post up. (2) moves quickly across the lane. (4), after passing to (1), moves away from the pass. See Diagram 2-3.

(3) delays until (2) has cleared the lane, and then cuts over (5) to the ballside post. See Diagram 2-4.

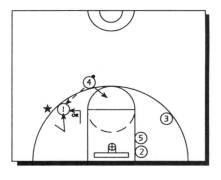

Diagram 2-3

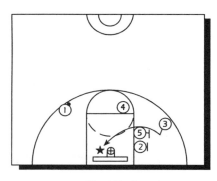

Shuffle Cut-1
Diagram 2-4

(4) completes the shuffle phase by screening for (5), who cuts to the point. See Diagram 2-5.

(1) screens down for (3), and (4) loops around (2) to again open up a double stack. See Diagram 2-6.

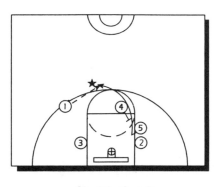

Shuffle Cut-Z
Diagram 2-5

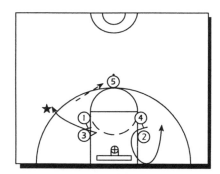

Double Stack
Diagram 2-6

At this point in the pattern, the coach has a decision to make. The coach may have the team restart the pattern via the UCLA slash, or omit it and go directly to the shuffle phase. Here are the two methods.

Restarting with the UCLA Slash

When (1) passes to (5) to conclude the pattern, (1) screens down for (3) and (4) loops around (2) after downscreening for (5) (Diagram 2-6). This forms a new double stack. When it opens up, (5) chooses to pass to (4). This keys (2) to move up to the high-post area and screen for (5). (5)'s dribble toward (4)'s side of the lane also tells (2) to move to the high post. See Diagrams 2-7 and 2-8.

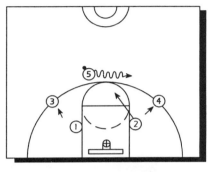

Strongside High Post
Diagram 2-7

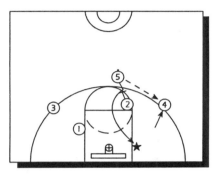

UCLA Slash
Diagram 2-8

(2) then pops out front to receive a pass from (4). From there, the UCLA phase is followed by the shuffle phase. See Diagrams 2-9 and 2-10.

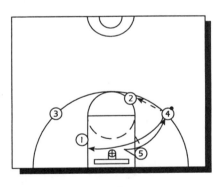

Pop Cut
Diagram 2-9

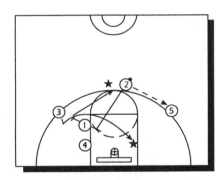

Shuffle 1,2
Diagram 2-10

Restarting Without the UCLA Phase

This time after (5) receives the pass from (1) and the stack opens up, (5) makes the entry pass (as to (4) in Diagram 2-11) but does not make the slash cut. (2) has made the downscreen and clears across the lane as (3) cuts over (1) to the ballside low post. At the same time, (5) moves away to screen for (1) to complete the shuffle phase. See Diagrams 2-11 and 2-12.

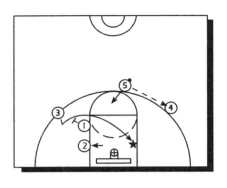

Diagram 2-11

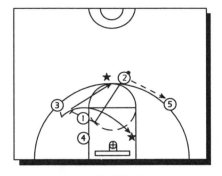

Shuffle 1, 2
Diagram 2-12

If (3) is not open, (4) passes to (1) and another sequence is keyed via the double stack. (5) loops around (2) as (4) downscreens for (3). See Diagram 2-13.

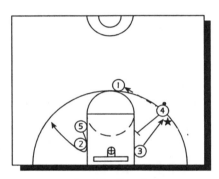

Double Stack
Diagram 2-13

So, in this second method, the UCLA slash cut is only run once, whereas in the former method, it initiates each new pattern sequence.

The Screen-and-Roll Play

The screen-and-roll play is an integral part of this offense and should be included early in the season. (1) keys it by passing to a wing (as to (2) in Diagram 2-14) and cutting down the lane *on the outside* of (4). This keys (4) to step out to (2) and set a screen. If (1) is not open, he or she clears across the lane.

(2) then dribbles off (4), as (1) loops around (3) and (5). (4) rolls after screening. This is done by using a *half-pivot*, rear turn as (2) dribbles by using the screen and shuffle-sliding to the basket after sealing defender X2 on your back if a "switch" is made by defenders X4 and X2. See Diagram 2-15.

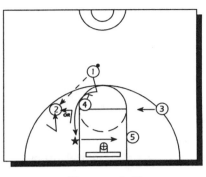

Diagram 2-14

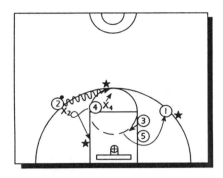

Diagram 2-15

(2) may shoot, hit (4) on the roll, or pass to (1) behind the double screen. (3), after screening, cuts across the lane and under (4) to the far wing position. (3) must delay long enough at the double screen to not get in the way of (4)'s "roll" option sliding down the lane to the basket. See Diagram 2-16.

(2) may then pass to either wing and restart the pattern in either of the two suggested ways. Diagram 2-17 shows the use of the UCLA slash cut, and Diagram 2-18 omits it and goes directly to the shuffle phase.

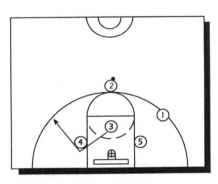

Diagram 2-16

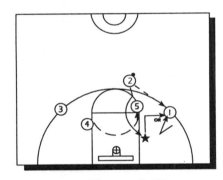

Diagram 2-17

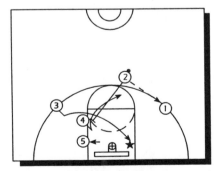

Diagram 2-18

This sequence allows a team to interject the screen-and-roll play, and return smoothly to the basic motion. It may also be used to initiate the screen-and-roll play.

A Backdoor Play

When defensive pressure is being used to deny passes to the wings, this backdoor play may be run. Diagram 2-19 shows (1) unable to pass to (2) or (3) who have made V- or L-cuts to get open. Seeing this, (4) breaks up above the free throw line and makes a jump stop as he or she receives a bounce pass from (1). (2) backdoors the defender, to become the first option. (5) moves toward (4)'s defender. (1) changes direction while cutting to become the second player through on a dovetail cut over (4) (Diagram 2-19).

If (2) is not open, (5) screens for (4), who pivots and faces the basket, then dribbles toward (3)'s side of the lane. (4) may shoot, hit (5) rolling, or pass to (2) as he or she comes around (3)'s downscreen. (1) finishes the second cutter through route at the wing position. See Diagram 2-20.

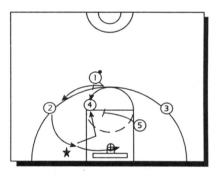

UCLA Backdoor
Diagram 2-19

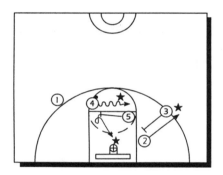

Diagram 2-20

The team can return to the basic pattern if (4) passes to (2). Diagrams 2-21 and 2-22 show (4) receiving the ball, (3) crossing the lane after downscreening, and (1) cutting to the ballside. This is followed by (4)'s second option downscreen for (5). (This example is without the UCLA option.)

Shuffle 1
Diagram 2-21

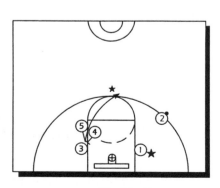

Shuffle 2
Diagram 2-22

Dribble Entry

Another way to handle defensive denial is via a dribble entry. Diagram 2-23 shows (1) dribbling at (2) and clearing (2) on a loop cut around (4) to the point. (4) then V-cuts into a low-post position.

(1) passes to (2) at the point, screens down for (4), who pops to the wing and then clears across the lane. See Diagram 2-24.

Dribble Entry
Diagram 2-23

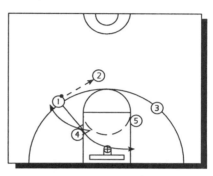

Pop Cut
Diagram 2-24

From there, the two-phase shuffle pattern is run. (3) cuts over (5) to the ballside low post (see Diagram 2-25), and (2) screens down for (5), who cuts to the point (see Diagram 2-26).

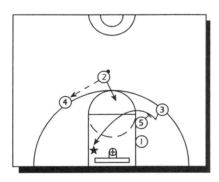

Shuffle 1
Diagram 2-25

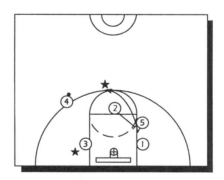

Shuffle 2
Diagram 2-26

These plays may be added when and if needed.

The Double Cut Play

(1) passes to (2) and makes a slash cut on the outside of (4). If (1) does not receive a return pass from (2), he or she clears across the lane. (3) waits until (1) clears the lane and then cuts over (5) to the ballside low post. See Diagram 2-27.

If (3) is not open, (4) pops out front and receives a pass from (2). (2) then screens down for (3) as (1) pops out of (5)'s downscreen on the other side. See Diagram 2-28.

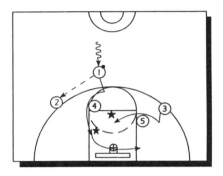

UCLA Double Slash Cut
Diagram 2-27

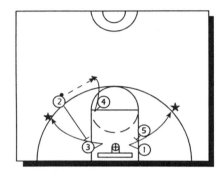

Pop Cuts
Diagram 2-28

This concludes a UCLA-type phase and it is followed by the shuffle phase. In Diagram 2-29, (4) passes to (1), (5) clears across the lane under (2), and the shuffle cuts by (3) and (2) follow.

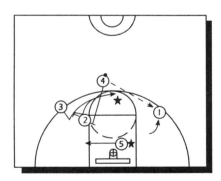

Shuffle 1, 2
Diagram 2-29

The Fake Outside Cut

One of UCLA's famous plays is the outside cut lob play. This play is an offshoot of it. Diagram 2-30 shows (1) passing to (2), and making an outside cut. This cut keys (5) to move to the ballside of the lane (short corner). (2) fakes to (1), and dribbles off (4), who has moved over to screen upon seeing the outside cut. (5) must clear the lane to make room for (4)'s roll.

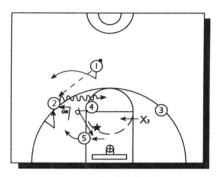

Fake Outside Cut
Diagram 2-30

(3)'s defender will usually drop in the lane to help on (4)'s penetration and (3) can choose either of two options. If X3's drop in the lane is free throw-line high, (3) can backdoor the defender. See Diagram 2-31. If the drop is below the free throw line, (3) can fake the backdoor and step out for a three-point opportunity. See Diagram 2-32.

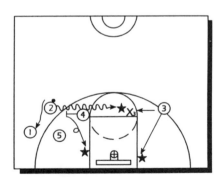

Screen Backdoor Roll
Diagram 2-31

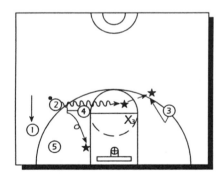

Screen Trey Roll
Diagram 2-32

This play provides an excellent opportunity to obtain a last shot because (2) can shoot, hit (4) on the roll, or pass to (3). It works very well if your offense includes the UCLA outside cut lob play. It may be run during this stacked UCLA shuffle offense anytime a stack opens up and a pass is made to a wing.

Zone Potential

This offense may be adapted to use against zone defenses in the form of two plays. They are the overload play and the triangle play.

The Overload Play

Diagram 2-33 shows point (1) pass to wing (2), and slash through to the ballside corner. (4) then steps out front on the zone perimeter and (3), the offside wing, cuts to the high-post area. This creates an overload on (2)'s side of the court.

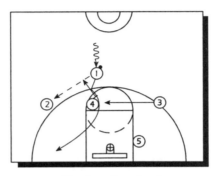

Slash to Overload
Diagram 2-33

The overload triangles are then utilized until (2) decides to switch sides. He or she does this by passing to (4) and screening the zone to permit (1) to move up to the wing area. After screening, (2) continues across the lane and under (5). See Diagrams 2-34 and 2-35.

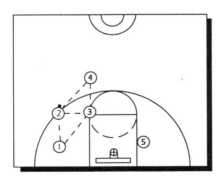

Overload
Diagram 2-34

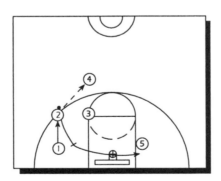

Switch Sides
Diagram 2-35

(4) helps (1) get open by ball faking a pass to the other side and then passing to (1). (4) then screens down for (5) to cut to the point as (3) slides down to the low-post area. See Diagram 2-36.

If (1) does not have a shot, (1) returns the ball out front to (5), and a new play sequence may be keyed. In Diagram 2-37, (5) keys an overload play on the other side by passing to (2) and slashing through to the ballside corner or short corner.

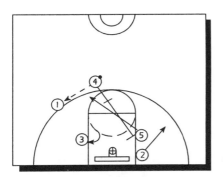

Screen Down
Diagram 2-36

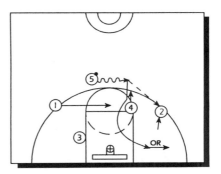

Slash to Overload
Diagram 2-37

The Triangle Play

The overload play tested the zone's perimeter, and the triangle play will now test its interior. Diagram 2-38 shows (1) pass to (2) and slash off (4). But this time, (1) cuts to the ballside low post (instead of the ballside corner). This cut keys the triangle play and tells (3) to cut to the middle of the zone as (4) pops out front.

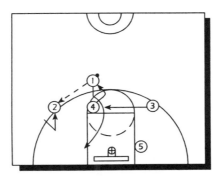

Slash to Triangle
Diagram 2-38

If (2) can pass to (3), (3) can shoot or drop the ball inside the zone to (1) or (5) for a power lay-up shot. See Diagram 2-39. Note (1) and (5) get open with a V-cut, muscle post move.

If (2) cannot get the ball to (3), (2) can pass to (4), and screen the zone to allow (1) to pop to the wing. See Diagram 2-40. Note that (2) continues across the lane after screening.

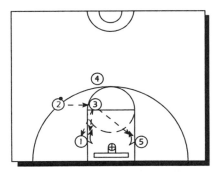

Diagram 2-39

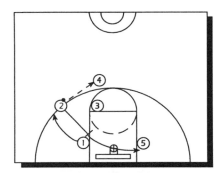

Screen the Zone
Diagram 2-40

(4) may then: (A) pass to (1) and screen down for (5) (see Diagram 2-41) or (B) pass to (2) and screen down for (3) (see Diagram 2-42).

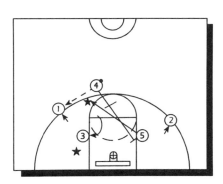

Screen Down
Diagram 2-41

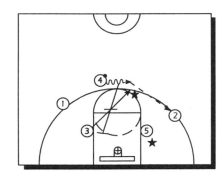

Screen Down
Diagram 2-42

Then once the ball is returned to the point, a new sequence may be keyed. In Diagram 2-43, (3) keys an overload by cutting to the corner or short corner, and in Diagrams 2-44, (3) keys a triangle play with a cut to the ballside low-post area.

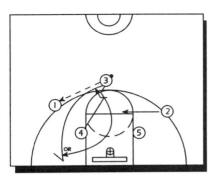

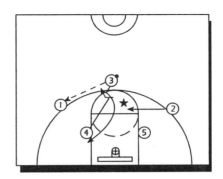

Slash to Overload
Diagram 2-43

Slash to Triangle
Diagram 2-44

These keys allow the two plays to be run interchangeably.

The stacked UCLA shuffle utilizes the stack, the UCLA slash cut, and the shuffle cuts. This combination of techniques gives it a lot of scoring potential. The fact that it may be adapted to use against zones gives it further value.

Outside Cut Variation

Previously, we used a fake outside cut in the stacked UCLA shuffle offense (Diagrams 2-30, 2-31, 2-32). In the event you especially like this option, you might consider this outside cut option to complement it.

Again the outside cut option is keyed by (1) passing to a wing ((3) in Diagram 2-45) and cutting over-the-top for a return pass/handoff from (3), (5) clears the lane to the ballside low post or short corner.

(4) moves up the lane and screens X3 as (3) cuts over the top for a lob. (2) cuts to the point as seen in Diagram 2-46.

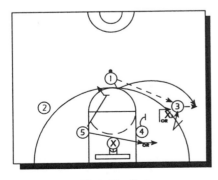

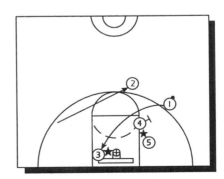

Outside Cut
Diagram 2-45

Over the Top
Diagram 2-46

The final phase of the outside cut options occurs as (4) steps out to screen for (1) on the pick-and-roll option. As this happens, (2) slides away to the opposite wing (Diagram 2-47). The shot options are for (1) if no switch occurs, to (4) on the roll if a defensive switch occurs, and for (2) if X2 cheats to help on (1). The outside cut is especially effective with (1) at the point because the pick and roll is between (1), a primary ball-handler and (4) or (5), primary screeners.

If no shot is produced, you are back in the basic set shown in Diagram 2-48. As (4) loops around (5)'s screen to cut to the wing.

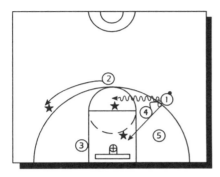

Screen and Roll
Diagram 2-47

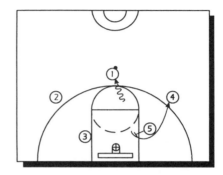

Diagram 2-48

CHAPTER 3

The Offside Stack Shuffle

This unique approach to the shuffle motion utilizes a point (1), two wings (2) and (3), and an offside stack with post (5) on top, and a good shooter (4) underneath. See Diagram 3-1.

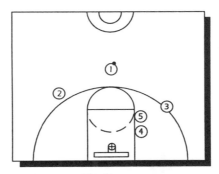

Offside Stack Set
Diagram 3-1

It consists of the basic motion with two variations, and the needed pressure relievers.

The Basic Motion

Diagram 3-2 shows the point (1) bringing the ball to the head of the key and entering it on the offside to wing (2). (1) then cuts down the lane on the stack side. (3) uses (1) and (5) to cut to the ballside post area. (4) uses (5), (1), and (3) to cut to the point. (1) is the first cutter, (3) the second cutter, and (4) is third.

If (3) is not open, (2) passes to (4) at the point. (5) screens down for (1)'s cut to the wing and then pops to the offside high post area, as (4) passes to (1). See Diagram 3-3.

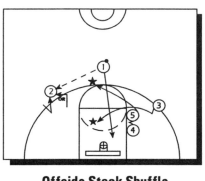

Offside Stack Shuffle
Diagram 3-2

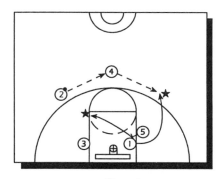

Reset
Diagram 3-3

(4) cuts down the lane and the pattern is repeated. See Diagrams 3-4 and 3-5.

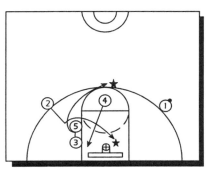

Offside Stack Shuffle
Diagram 3-4

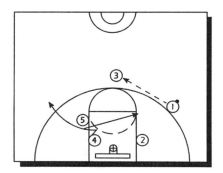

Reset
Diagram 3-5

The Post Comeback Variation

It soon becomes obvious that there are no scoring options for (5). To prevent (5)'s defender from jamming the middle, the post comeback variation may be run. Diagram 3-6 shows the pattern at a point where (5) has performed his or her screening functions and is moving to form a new double screen on the side away from the ball.

Note in Diagram 3-6 that (5)'s defender, X5, feels safe to step out and hedge on (1)'s cut over the double screen. Seeing this, (5) back pivots toward X4 until making contact with X5, extends his or her elbows, and raises his or her hands in a receiving position (palms facing the ball). This wide stance makes it difficult for X5 to get back into a functional defensive position, as (5) doubles back to the ballside low post area for a pass from (4) and an unmolested lay-up shot.

If (5) is not open, (5) moves high as (1) comes to the ballside and (2) cuts to the point off of (3) and (1). See Diagram 3-7.

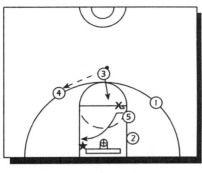

Post Comeback
Diagram 3-6

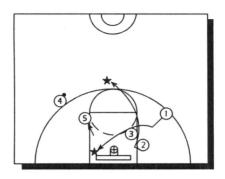

Reset
Diagram 3-7

(4) then passes to (2), and the play continues. See Diagrams 3-8 and 3-9.

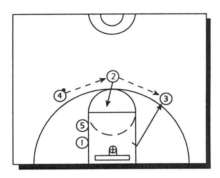

Diagram 3-8

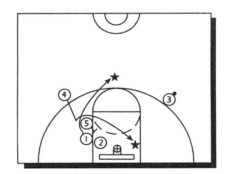

Offside Stack Shuffle
Diagram 3-9

Strongside Play

When the ball cannot be entered on the weakside, (1) passes to the strongside wing (3) and makes an outside cut. (3) handoff returns the ball and cuts over (5) to the weakside lay-up area for a possible lob pass. See Diagram 3-10.

If (3) is not open, the ball is reversed to (3) at the wing position by (2), who has moved to the point. See Diagram 3-11.

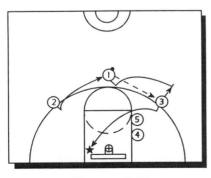

Diagram 3-10

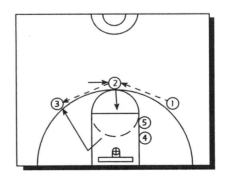

Diagram 3-11

From there, the basic pattern is run. See Diagram 3-12.

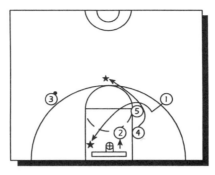

Diagram 3-12

Pressure Relievers

"Quick" Option

When defensive pressure is preventing passes to the wings, the "quick" option may be run. In Diagram 3-13, (1) cannot pass to (2) or (3), so (1) dribbles toward (3) and this keys (3) to cut over (5). If (3) is not open, (5) downscreens for (4), who pops to the wing and receives a pass from (1).

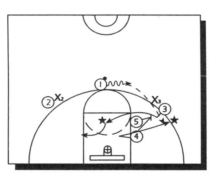

Diagram 3-13

(5) then crosses the lane to form the double screen with (3), and the basic pattern is run. See Diagrams 3-14 and 3-15.

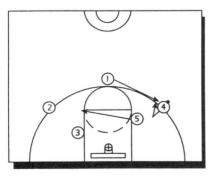

Diagram 3-14

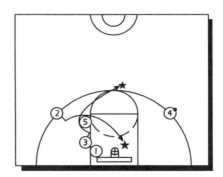

Diagram 3-15

It is also a good change-up on this play for (2) to cut early and low off (3), as (5) is crossing the lane. See Diagram 3-16.

From there, the basic pattern proceeds in its usual manner. See Diagram 3-17.

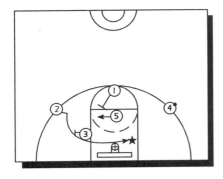

Early Shuffle
Diagram 3-16

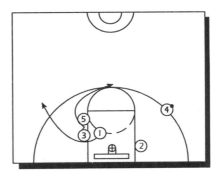

Diagram 3-17

Weakside Dribble Entry

Since the basic pattern is keyed with a weakside entry, it helps when the defense is denying the pass to utilize a dribble entry on that side. In Diagram 3-18, (1) cannot pass to (2) so (1) dribbles at (2), who clears across the lane. In effect, this key simply changes the assignments of players (1) and (2).

As soon as (2) has cleared the lane, (3) cuts over (5), and the pattern continues. It helps if (1) keeps the dribble alive until (3) has completed the cut. See Diagram 3-19.

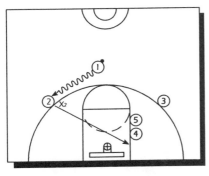

Weakside Dribble Entry
Diagram 3-18

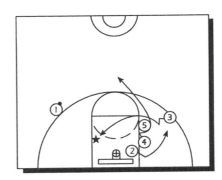

Diagram 3-19

The quick play and the weakside dribble entry play are necessary components of this basic offensive plan, and must be taught early in the season. The following secondary plays may be added when and if needed.

Strongside Lob Play

The basic strongside play is keyed by a pass to the wing and an outside cut. The strongside lob play takes advantage of (1)'s defender's tendency to anticipate (1)'s cut and beat him or her to the spot. In Diagram 3-20, (1) passes to the strongside wing, takes two steps toward (3), and then cuts back off (2)'s screen to the weakside lay-up area for a possible lob pass from (3).

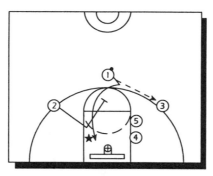

Strongside Fake to Lob
Diagram 3-20

If (1) is not open, (2) steps to the point, receives the ball from (3), and reverses it to (1). See Diagram 3-21.

From there, the basic pattern may continue. See Diagram 3-22.

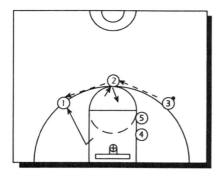

Diagram 3-21

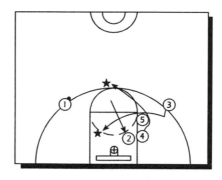

Diagram 3-22

Wing Lob Backdoor Play

Once you have run the preceding play, the wing lob play should work well. In Diagram 3-23, (2) starts up to screen for (1) and X2 hedges on (1)'s cut. This allows (2) to backdoor X2 and receive the lob pass.

Also note that (1) faked the lob cut. This move gets (1) open in the event (2) is not open for the lob. Then the basic pattern may be run. See Diagram 3-24.

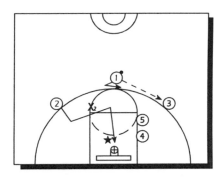

Lob Backdoor
Diagram 3-23

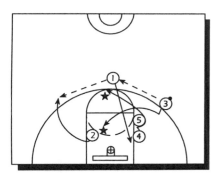

Offside Stack Shuffle
Diagram 3-24

Weakside Screen and Roll

Another way to initiate the basic pattern on the weakside is through a screen and roll. In Diagram 3-25, (1) receives a screen from (2) and dribbles to the weakside wing as (2) rolls down the lane.

As soon as (2) clears the lane, (3) cuts and the basic pattern is run. Again, it helps if (1) does not pick up the dribble, at least until (3) cuts. See Diagram 3-26.

Weakside Screen and Roll
Diagram 3-25

Offside Stack Shuffle
Diagram 3-26

A Two-Player Front Pattern Set

If a team wants to run this offense but lacks a strong point guard, they may initiate the basic pattern from a two-player front. Diagram 3-27 shows (1) pass to (3) and cross in front of (2) to screen for the offside forward (4). (2) uses (1)'s cut and (5)'s position to slash to the ballside post area. (4) uses (1)'s screen to come to the point and then (5) swings to the ballside high post area.

The ball is then reversed to (1) via (4), and the basic pattern is run. See Diagram 3-28.

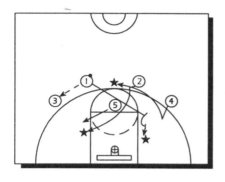

Two-Guard Entry
Diagram 3-27

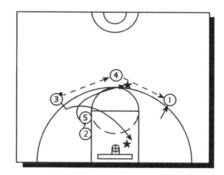

Offside Stack Shuffle
Diagram 3-28

Zone Potential

Even to Odd

The first step is to change the perimeter from even to odd. This is done by first passing the ball around the four-player perimeter with a hope that this puts an adjusting zone defenses in a two-player front (2-3 or 2-1-2). See Diagram 3-29.

Then the offense converts to its basic odd front. Diagram 3-30 shows (1) pass to (3) and cut over (5) to screen for (4), who moves to the point. (5) then swings to the ballside and the team is in its stack shuffle set.

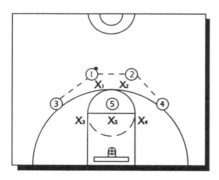

Even Front
Diagram 3-29

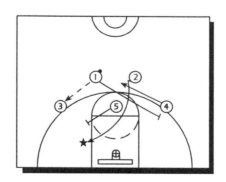

Odd Front
Diagram 3-30

One Pop to the Point Versus Zones

The pattern is then run, but the low player in the stack, (4), pops to the point after the ball is reversed and stays there until its conclusion.

Diagram 3-31 shows (3) pass to (4), who reverses it to (1). (4) cuts down the middle, (3) breaks to the free throw line area, and (2) pops to the point.

(1) can: (A) pass to (3) in the middle of the zone. (3) could then pass to (5) down low or to (4), looping around (5) to the offside wing. See Diagram 3-32.

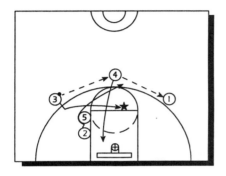

Diagram 3-31

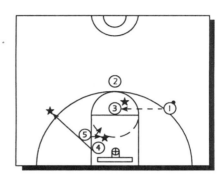

Pop to Point
Diagram 3-32

(B) pass to (5), breaking high after (3) drops down to the low post. (5) can then shoot, look inside for (3), or reverse the ball to (4). See Diagram 3-33.

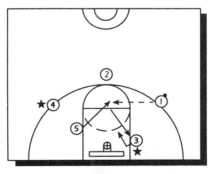

Diagram 3-33

(C) throws crosscourt to (4) for three points, or (D) reverses the ball to (4) via point guard (2). From there, the pattern may be run. See Diagrams 3-34 through 3-36.

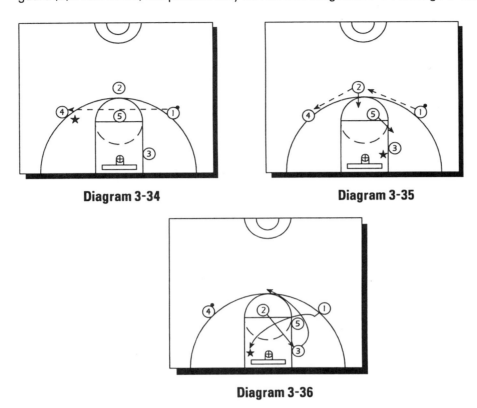

Diagram 3-34

Diagram 3-35

Diagram 3-36

Please note that (2) stayed at the point once the play was initiated. That is why versus zones, the offense is called "one pop to the point versus zones."

The Overload Phase Via a Dribble Entry

Diagram 3-37 shows the point (1) dribbling at weakside wing (2), and pushing him or her to the corner. This key also tells the off-side wing (3) to cut to the high-post area, as (4) pops to the point.

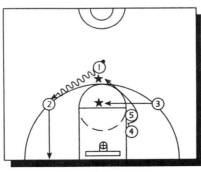

Zone Dribble Entry
Diagram 3-37

(1) can then:

(A) pass to (3), who can shoot or look inside for (5).

(B) utilize the overload triangles. See Diagram 3-38.

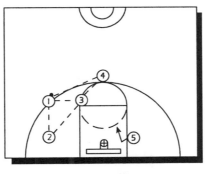

Overload
Diagram 3-38

(C) wait for (2) to clear the corner and look for (5) breaking high as (3) breaks to the low post. See Diagram 3-39.

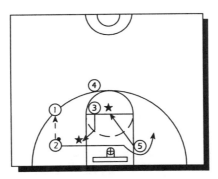

Corner Clear
Diagram 3-39

(D) reverse it to (2) via (4), and run the play on that side. See Diagram 3-40.

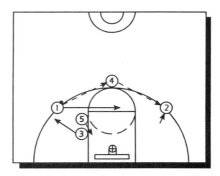

Reverse and Reset
Diagram 3-40

Note: When (4) received the ball at the point, (4) could have keyed another corner push overload by dribbling at the weakside wing (2). See Diagram 3-41.

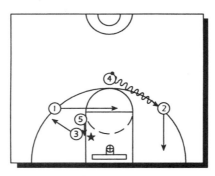

Diagram 3-41

This two-play zone offense allows a team to test the zone's middle and corner. These are the most vulnerable areas of many zone defenses.

The offside stack shuffle presents a new way to screen away, and then screen down. It is designed for a team with a big player whose greatest strength is rebounding, and four mobile perimeter players. The plan enables a team to keep (5) inside and still run a shuffle-type pattern.

CHAPTER 4

A UCLA Continuity

This offense consists of a basic UCLA-type continuity with two variations to keep the defense guessing. It is run from a 1-3-1 high-low post set that tends to keep the big players inside. The ideal personnel to run it would have two big inside and three mobile perimeter players.

The Basic UCLA Motion

Diagram 4-1 shows the point (1) enter the ball to (2), with the wing on the high-post side. Player (1) then makes a UCLA slashcut off post (4) to the ballside low-post area. This tells (4) to screen away for (3), who cuts to the point. Also note that (1)'s cut was inside of (4).

(2) passes to (3) at the point and screens down for (1), who pops to the wing. (2) does not delay as he crosses the lane and under (5). See Diagram 4-2 .

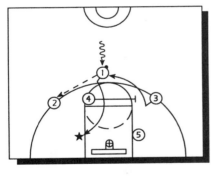

Slash Cut Entry
Diagram 4-1

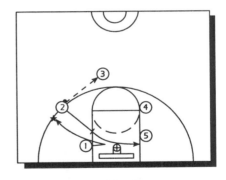

Pop Cut
Diagram 4-2

(4) then rolls back to the ballside low post after (3) passes to (1). See Diagram 4-3.

If (1) is not open, (3) dribbles toward the other side. This tells (4) to go to the offside low-post area, (2) to pop out off (5)'s downscreen, and (5) to move up to the high post. See Diagram 4-4.

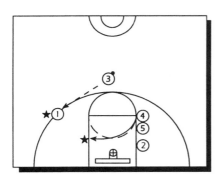

Diagram 4-3

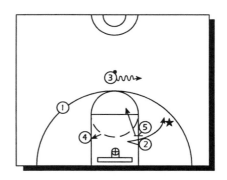

Reset Change of Sides
Diagram 4-4

This dribbling by (3) keys the change of sides, and creates a better passing angle for the pass to (2). The motion is then repeated on that side. See Diagrams 4-5 through 4-8.

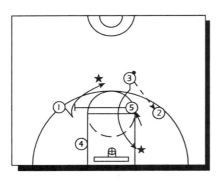

Slash and Screen Away
Diagram 4-5

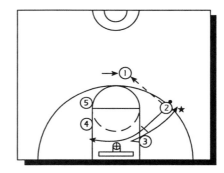

Pop Cut
Diagram 4-6

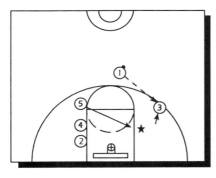

Diagram 4-7

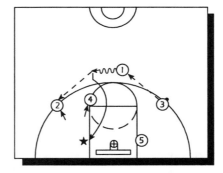

Diagram 4-8

During this motion, (4) and (5) are the primary rebounders and the player at the point, usually (1), (2), or (3), has the primary responsibility as the safety for defensive balance.

Basic Play Variations

Dribble Entry Lob

The dribble entry lob play is used to relieve pressure and as a key to a pattern variation for this offense.

In Diagram 4-9, (1) seeing that (2) is being denied the entry pass, dribbles at and clears (2) to the ballside low-post area. This keys (4) to screen away for (3) (just as the slash play did in the basic play). But this time, (5) cuts to the ballside high-post area.

(5)'s clearout allows (4) to roll to the offside low-post area for a possible lob pass from (1). See Diagram 4-10.

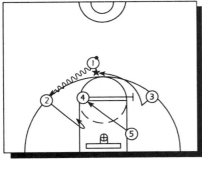

Dribble Entry
Diagram 4-9

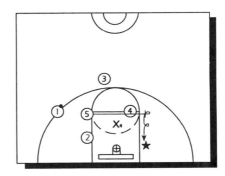

Lob
Diagram 4-10

This variation from the basic play works well because X4 anticipates (4)'s roll back to the ballside low-post area (as per the basic play) and assumes a position to "plug" the cut across the lane.

If (1) cannot pass to (4), (1) passes to (3) at the point and the basic slash cut entry is run at the opposite side. See Diagrams 4-11 through 4-13.

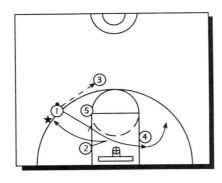

Diagram 4-11

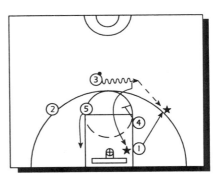

Slash Entry
Diagram 4-12

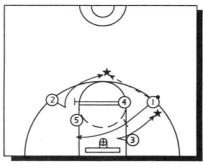

Diagram 4-13

The point must be taught to set up on a particular side and not in the middle. This tells the ballside post to set up high and the offside post to play the low post.

Post-to-Point Variation

(1) passes to (2) and slashes off (4) to the low post, and (4) screens away for (3). But this time, (3) cuts low and away from the screen. This keys (4) to pop to the point. See Diagram 4-14.

(2) passes to (4) at the point and downscreens for (1), who cuts to the wing. (4)'s cut to the point often results in being open, so (4) should catch the ball in an all-purpose position. See Diagram 4-15.

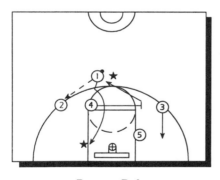

**Post to Point
Diagram 4-14**

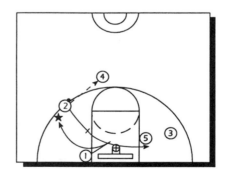

Diagram 4-15

If (4) does not have a shot, he or she returns the ball to (1)'s side. In that case, (1) may shoot, or pass to (3), coming over the double screen of (2) and (5) to the ballside low post. See Diagram 4-16.

If (1) cannot shoot or pass to (3), (1) returns the ball to (4) and restarts the play. See Diagram 4-17.

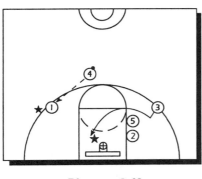

Diagram 4-16

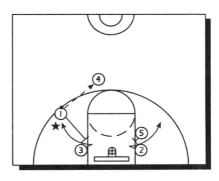

Diagram 4-17

If (4) is being denied the pass, (1) can dribble-clear (4) to restart the motion. See Diagrams 4-18 and 4-19.

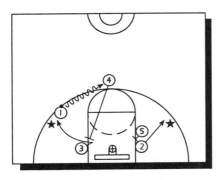

Dribble Clear Reset
Diagram 4-18

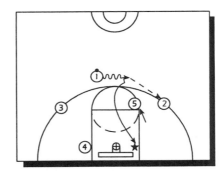

Slash Entry
Diagram 4-19

These two play variations are an integral part of the offense. During the early part of the season, you must teach the basic pattern, the dribble entry lob, and the post-to-point play. Otherwise, this pattern is too predictable and easy to defend.

Pressure Relievers

The primary pressure reliever for this offense is the dribble entry lob play. However, if an additional one is needed, the backdoor wheel play may be used.

The Backdoor Wheel Play

This play begins when (1), seeing that (2) is being overplayed, bounce passes to (4). (2) backdoors the defender and is the first option. If (2) is not open, (1) makes a change of direction and becomes the second player through on a dovetail cut (see Diagram 4-20). At that point, (4) has two primary options after the backdoor look to (2): (A) may pass to (1). When this happens, (1) attempts to penetrate. When (1) is stopped, the offside wing (3) cuts over (5), as (2), who has crossed the lane, cuts under. See Diagram 4-21.

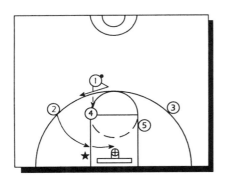

Diagram 4-20

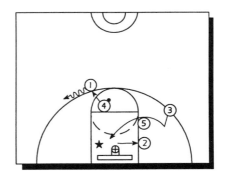

Dovetail handoff
Diagram 4-21

After handing off to (1), (4) screens away for (5), who cuts to the point. See Diagram 4-22.

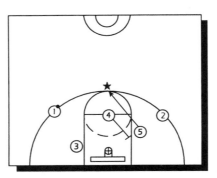

Diagram 4-22

(B) (4)'s other option is to fake to (1), take one dribble in the opposite direction, and pass to (2) behind the double screen of (5) and (3). ((3) does not cut across the lane unless (4) hands off to (1).) After (4) passes to (2), (4) screens away for (1), who pops to the free throw line. See Diagrams 4-23 and 4-24.

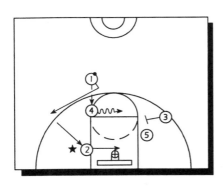

Diagram 4-23

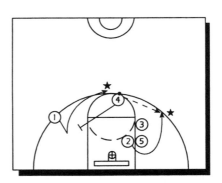

Double Screen
Diagram 4-24

Secondary Plays

These plays may be added when and if needed.

The Lob, Lob Play

This play is distinguishable from the basic motion because the ball is entered on the side opposite the high post. In Diagram 4-25, (1) passes to the wing (3) and cuts off high post (4) for a possible lob pass. (5) uses this opportunity to post up on the defender. Also note that (3) came to meet this fairly dangerous entry pass.

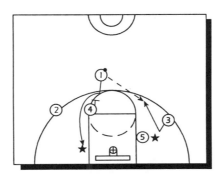

Weakside Entry
Diagram 4-25

If (1) is not open, (2) steps toward the baseline and V-cuts off (4) to the point. (4) stepped out to facilitate the screen. (2) can shoot, pass inside to (5) on a seal move, or reverse the ball to (1). See Diagram 4-26. In Diagram 4-27, (2) reverses the ball to (1). This keys (5) to back screen for (4), who back pivots and rolls to the basket for a possible lob pass.

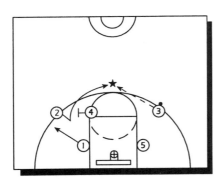

Diagram 4-26

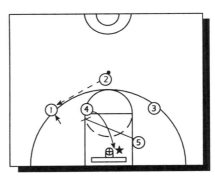

Lob Cut
Diagram 4-27

If (4) is not open, (2) cuts off (5), and the basic UCLA pattern is run. See Diagram 4-28.

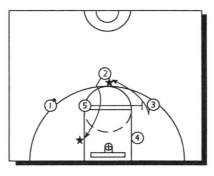

Slash Entry
Diagram 4-28

The Guard Loop Play

This play may be run to get a last shot for (1), or to take advantage of a weak defender on (5). Diagram 4-29 shows (1) pass to wing (2), and cut through on the outside of (4). This cut distinguishes the guard loop play from the basic UCLA play. (2) looks first for (1), and then for (5), coming to the ballside over a screen by (1).

If neither is open, (4) screens down for (1), who loops back to the point. This screen works particularly well if X1 "hedged" on (5)'s cut low across the lane. See Diagram 4-30.

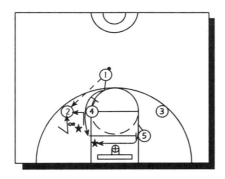

Slash Outside Cut
Diagram 4-29

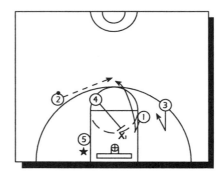

Diagram 4-30

If (5) is being fronted, (2) may pass to (4), popping back to the high post after screening for (1). (4) then may be able to get the ball inside to (5) on a seal move. See Diagram 4-31.

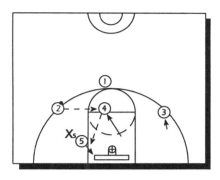

Diagram 4-31

However, in most cases, the pass is made to (1) at the point, who shoots or reverses the ball to (3), and repeats the guard loop play. See Diagrams 4-32 and 4-33.

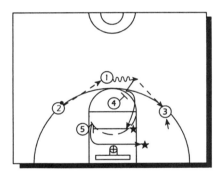

**Slash Outside Cut
Diagram 4-32**

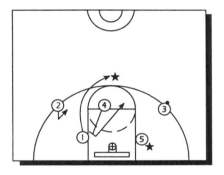

Diagram 4-33

Coaching Point:
When (1) restarted the guard loop play, (1) could have called the basic UCLA pattern by cutting inside (or basket side) of (4) (see Diagram 4-34). This is up to the coach, and the keys must be solidified in practice.

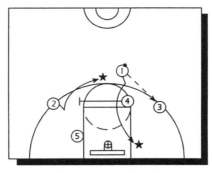

Diagram 4-34

Zone Potential

The best zone potential found in this offense can be utilized by running the UCLA slash play like the dribble entry lob play. Diagram 4-35 shows (1) pass to the wing (2), and slash to the low-post area. (4) then screens away for (3) and rolls to the low post as (5) breaks to the ballside high post.

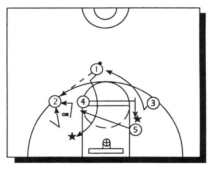

Diagram 4-35

Triangle Play
At this point, if (2) can pass to (5), either (1) or (4) may be open inside the zone. See Diagram 4-36.

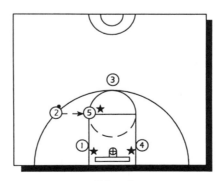

Triangle
Diagram 4-36

Overload

If (5) is not open, (1) breaks to the corner or short corner and the ball is moved around the overload triangles until (2) wishes to reset the offense. See Diagram 4-37.

(2) does so by passing to the point (as to (3) in Diagram 4-38) and cutting down and across the lane to a position under (4). Versus zones, (2) does not screen for (1).

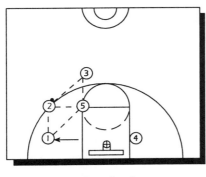

Overload
Diagram 4-37

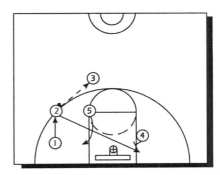

Change Sides
Diagram 4-38

(3) may then dribble toward the opposite side to key (4) to move up to the high post and (2) to cut to the wing. The motion is then repeated. See Diagrams 4-39 through 4-42.

Slash
Diagram 4-39

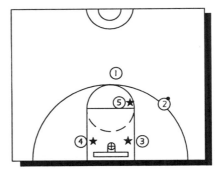

Overload
Diagram 4-40

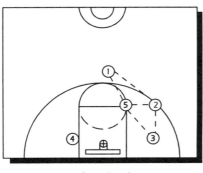

Overload
Diagram 4-41

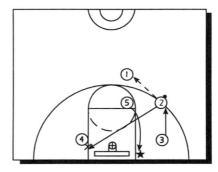

Change Sides
Diagram 4-42

The zone offense provides a triangle play, an overload, and a screened ball reversal.

This UCLA type of continuity provides many of John Wooden's famous shot options within the context of enough player movement to counter today's pressure and help player defenses. It offers both quick shot opportunities, and the ability to run the motion until the clock shows the appropriate amount of time, and then obtain a high-percentage shot. The fact that it may be adapted for use against zones gives it further value.

The Stack Overload Pattern

The stack overload pattern is initiated from a 1-2-2 set. It has the unique feature of spreading out the defense by utilizing the deep ballside corner.

The basic pattern is designed for a team with two big players and three mobile perimeter players. It is helpful if one of the big players is a strong outside or three-point shooter.

A team using this offensive plan should expect to start the season prepared to run the basic pattern, the reset play, and two basic pattern variations, which are the quick lob and the wing loop. If they expect to encounter a great deal of defensive pressure that denies play-initiating entry passes, a dribble-entry play might be added.

The Basic Pattern

Diagram 5-1 shows the double stack open up with (2) and (3) popping to the wings off the downscreens of posts (4) and (5). Point (1) can then pass to either wing (as to (2) in Diagram 5-1). (1) hesitates at the point as the ballside post (4) posts up.

If (2) cannot get the ball inside to (4), (4) clears to three-point range in the ballside corner. This keys (1) to screen away for (3), who cuts to the point. See Diagram 5-2.

Double Stack Popout
Diagram 5-1

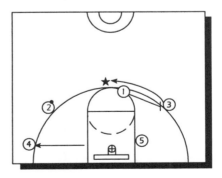

Diagram 5-2

(2) then has two options. (2) may: (A) pass to (4) in the corner and run the stack overload pattern, or (B) if (4) is being denied the pass, reset the double stack by passing to (3) at the point.

Option A: The Stack Overload
In Diagram 5-3, (2) passes to (4) in the corner and screens for (3) at the point. The subsequent cut down the lane by (3) will work best if (2) cuts toward the lane and then up to (3)'s defender, and if (3) will make a jab step to left before the cut.

If (3) is not open, (3) clears across the lane and under (5). This keys (1) to fake toward the baseline and cut over (5)'s definite screen to the ballside low-post area. See Diagram 5-4.

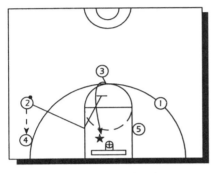

Stack Overload
Diagram 5-3

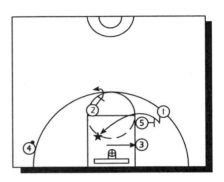

Diagram 5-4

If (4) cannot pass to (1), he or she dribbles toward the point and passes to (2), who screened for (3) and popped to the ballside of the point. See Diagram 5-5.

A new double stack is then initiated with (4) screening down for (1), as (5) screens for (3). See Diagram 5-6.

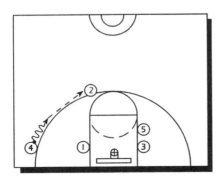

Diagram 5-5

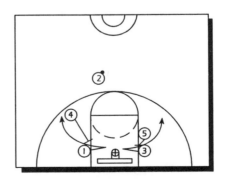

Double Stack Popout
Diagram 5-6

This new stack overload pattern begins with big players (4) and (5) back in their inside post-up positions.

Option B: The Reset Play

Diagram 5-7 takes place at a juncture where (2) and (3) have cut to the wings, (1) has passed to (2), and (4) has posted up and then cut to the corner. Seeing that (2) cannot pass to (4), (1) quickly screens away for (3), who cuts to the point. See Diagram 5-8.

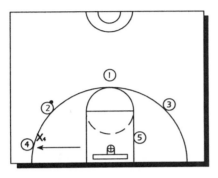

Diagram 5-7

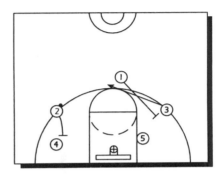

Diagram 5-8

(2) passes to (3) and screens for (4), as (1) screens down for (5). Both screeners roll to their respective low-post positions, as both inside players cut to the wings. (3) can then pass to either wing (as to (5) in Diagram 5-9) and restart the pattern.

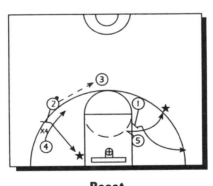

Reset
Diagram 5-9

From there, (2) and (1) will post up then (1) will cut to the corner, and the same two options will be available to (5).

Basic Pattern Variations

The Quick Lob Play

Diagram 5-10 shows the point (1) passing to (2), coming off (4)'s downscreen. As (4) posts up low, the defender will front (4), or at least use a strong three-fourths overplay. At that point, (5) cuts to the high-post area. If (2) can get the ball to (5), it will change the passing angle to (4). (4) can then back pivot into the defender and seal to receive a pass from (5) for a power lay-up shot. The pass should be a bounce pass or a "hanging" lob pass.

If (2) cannot pass to (4) or (5), (4) clears to the corner or short corner. This key tells (1), who hesitated and jab stepped toward (2), to cut off (5) to the offside lay-up area for a possible lob pass. This pass should be thrown with enough arch that would allow it to hit inbounds if no one touches it. High-line drive-type passes are very hard to catch in this situation. See Diagram 5-11.

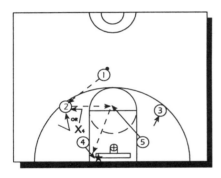

Diagram 5-10

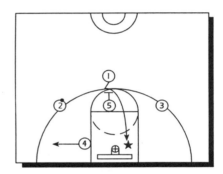

Quick Lob
Diagram 5-11

If (1) is not open, (2) passes to (4) in the corner and screens for (5) at the point. From that point, the play proceeds as before, but with (1) and (5) changing assignments. See Diagrams 5-12 through 5-14.

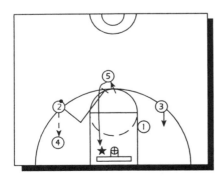

Stack Overload
Diagram 5-12

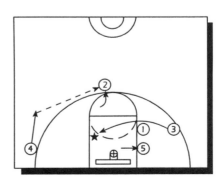

Diagram 5-13

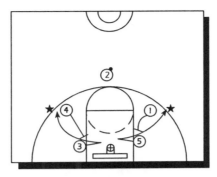

Double Stack Popout
Diagram 5-14

This variation is particularly helpful when (5)'s defender has been dominating the lane by blocking shots and/or rebounding. It puts X5 on the perimeter and involves him or her in play situations.

The Wing Loop Play

This play starts out like the basic motion. (1) passes to (2) coming out of the stack, (4) posts up and then clears to the corner. See Diagram 5-15.

However, this time when (2) passes to (4) in the corner and (1) screens away for (3), (3) cuts all the way to the basket. (1) then makes a replacement cut to the point. See Diagram 5-16.

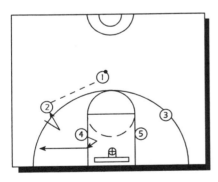

Diagram 5-15

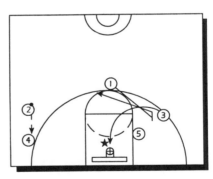

Wing Loop
Diagram 5-16

If (3) is not open, (3) clears to the offside wing and (2) screens for (1) at the point. See Diagram 5-17.

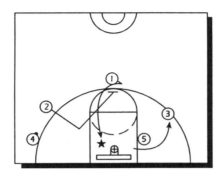

Stack Overload
Diagram 5-17

From there, the pattern proceeds as before. See Diagram 5-18 and 5-19.

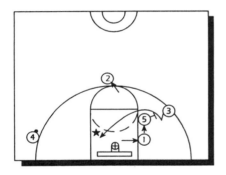

Diagram 5-18

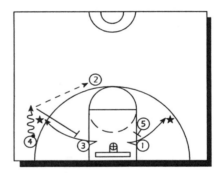

Double Stack Popout
Diagram 5-19

Pressure Relievers

When this entry pass to start the basic pattern is being denied, (1) may resort to a dribble entry. Here are two examples:

The Dribble-Entry Rotation
In Diagram 5-20, the point (1) cannot pass to either wing because of defensive denials. Seeing this, (1) dribbles at and clears (2) on a push to the corner. This tells (4) to clear the ballside post and cut around (5). (3), the offside wing, takes the point.

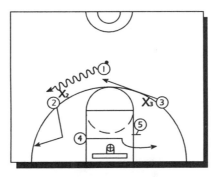

Dribble Entry Corner Push
Diagram 5-20

After this player rotation, (1) has two options. He or she can pass to (2) in the corner and run the pattern (see Diagram 5-21), or pass to (3) at the point and initiate a new double stack. See Diagram 5-22.

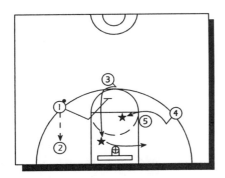

Stack Overload
Diagram 5-21

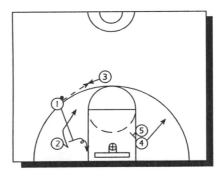

Double Stack Popout
Diagram 5-22

The Dribble-Entry Loop

Seeing that the wings are being denied the entry pass, (1) dribbles at and clears (2) down and around post (4) using a loop cut to the point. See Diagram 5-23. (1) should keep the dribble alive.

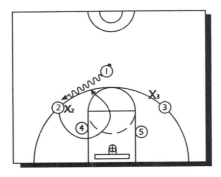

Diagram 5-23

(1)'s two options at the point are: (A) to continue the pattern by passing to (4) in the corner (see Diagram 5-24), or (B) passing to (2) at the point and restarting the offense with a new double stack. See Diagram 5-25.

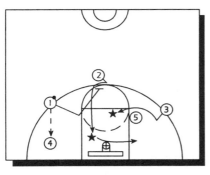

Stack Overload
Diagram 5-24

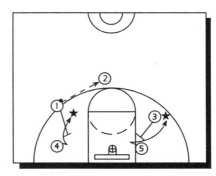

Double Stack Popout
Diagram 5-25

The second options really reshuffles the deck by putting both posts ((4) and (5)), and their big defenders on the perimeter.

Secondary Plays

The Outside Cut Lob

In Diagram 5-26, (1) passes to (2) and makes an outside cut. This tells the ballside post (4) to clear to the corner, and the offside post (5) to cut to the ballside high-post area.

(2) returns the ball to (1) on a handoff pass and cuts over (5) to the offside of the lane for a possible lob pass. See Diagram 5-27.

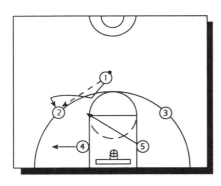

Outside Cut
Diagram 5-26

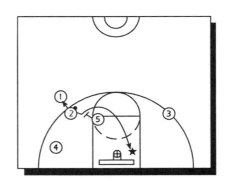

Handoff Lob
Diagram 5-27

If (2) is not open, (5) moves to the point, (1) passes to (4), and the basic motion is run. See Diagrams 5-28 and 5-29.

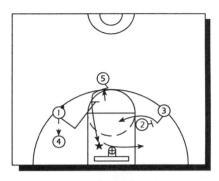

**Stack Overload
Diagram 5-28**

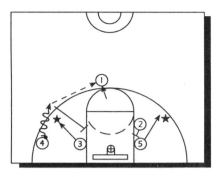

**Double Stack Popout
Diagram 5-29**

If (4) had been covered, (1) could have passed to (5) at the point and reset a double stack to again initiate the basic stack overload motion. See Diagram 5-30.

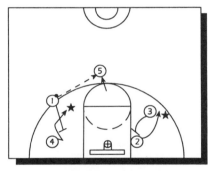

Diagram 5-30

Flexing Out the Big Defenders

When the opposition's big defenders are dominating the inside, the flex pattern may be used to keep them busy. Diagram 5-31 shows the point (1) calling the flex by dribbling toward (2)'s side. This tells the offside post (5) to break to the offside head of the key and receive a pass.

(4) sets up "above the block" and screens for (2), who cuts across the lane. See Diagram 5-32.

From that point, you can have your team run either of two play options. You can (A) continue the flex, or (B) reset the double stack.

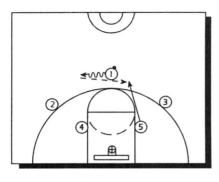

Diagram 5-31

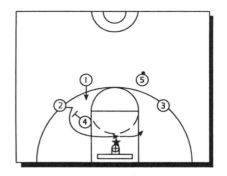

Diagram 5-32

(A) Continuing the Flex

After (1) passes to (5), screens down for (4), and the flex continues. See Diagram 5-33.

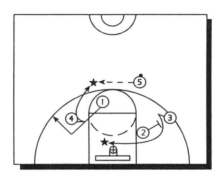

Diagram 5-33

(B) Resetting the Double Stack

Diagram 5-34 shows (1) pass to (5) and (2) make the flex cut.

If (2) is not open and you desire to reset the double stack to restart the basic pattern, (1) screens down for (4) and rolls inside, as (3) screens down for (2). See Diagram 5-35.

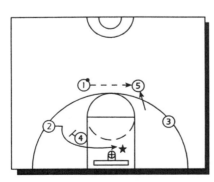

Break the Flex
Diagram 5-34

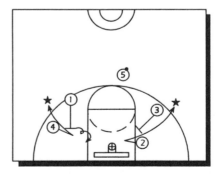

Double Stack Reset
Diagram 5-35

(5) may then pass to either wing to restart the stack overload motion.

The Shuffle
The stack overload set is an ideal alignment from which to run a shuffle. Once the ballside post ((4) in Diagram 5-36) has cut to the corner or short corner, (2) can start the shuffle by passing to (3) at the point. (3) then reverses it to (1) at the offside wing. (5) reads the key and cuts to the ballside high-post area.

(2) slashes off (5) and (4) replaces him at the wing. See Diagram 5-37.

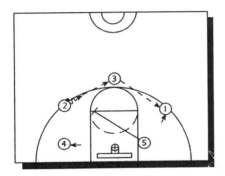

Diagram 5-36

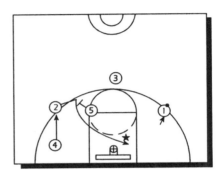

Shuffle Cut
Diagram 5-37

(5) steps up to allow (3) to cut to the offside lay-up area for a possible lob pass. See Diagram 5-38.

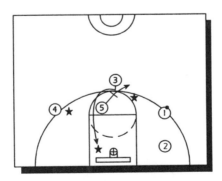

Lob Cut
Diagram 5-38

Note that (4) is in the three-point area in case X4 sags to help on the lob pass. This skip pass option to (4) must be pointed out to (1) in practice.

From that point, (2) can post up and then cut to the corner. Then a pass to (5) would key the shuffle (see Diagram 5-39) and a pass to (2) would key the stack overload options (see Diagram 5-40).

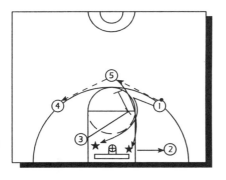

Diagram 5-39

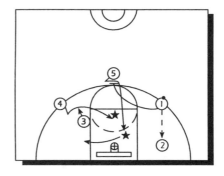

**Shuffle Lob
Diagram 5-40**

This combination requires a lot of coaching, but the final product is very difficult to defense.

The Stack Overload Plus the Mixer Pattern
The stack overload will also work very well in conjunction with the mixer passing game motion.

Diagrams 5-41 and 5-42 show the mixer in motion.

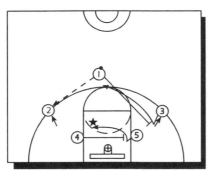

**Mixer
Diagram 5-41**

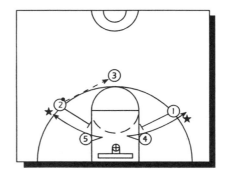

Diagram 5-42

In Diagram 5-43, (2) calls the stack overload by breaking to the corner or short corner as (5) receives a pass at the wing. (3) screens away for (4).

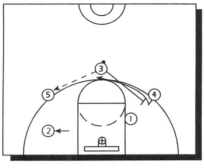

Diagram 5-43

(5) passes to (2) in the corner and screens for (4) at the point. The stack overload options are then run. See Diagrams 5-44 and 5-45.

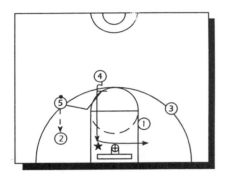

Diagram 5-44

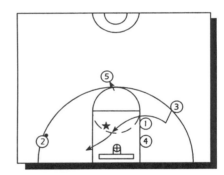

Diagram 5-45

If neither option is open, (2) dribbles out toward the wing and passes to (5), who popped high and to the ballside after screening for (4). See Diagram 5-46.

The mixer is now back in operation until another stack overload play is called via a cut to the ballside corner by the ballside low post. See Diagram 5-47.

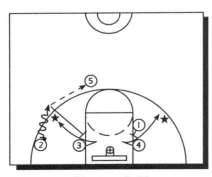

Diagram 5-46

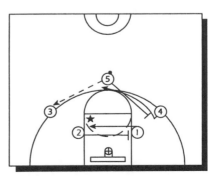

Diagram 5-47

Zone Potential

The basic zone motion for this offense is the guard loop play. Against zones, this play attempts to trap the zone inside, overloads it, tests its middle, and then utilizes a screened ball reversal.

The Guard Loop Play Versus Zones

Diagram 5-48 shows the double stack open up and wings (2) and (3) popping to their floor positions. Note that against zones, big players (4) and (5) started at wing positions before screening down. Since most zones defend from the inside out, this maneuver helps the posts trap the zone inside. In their scramble to cover the wings, the zone defenders may not maintain proper spacing and this may allow (1) to pass directly inside to one of the big players ((4) or (5)). Remember, the rule in downscreens is screen, step up to the ball, and post-up.

Diagram 5-48

However, in most cases, (1) passes to a wing (as to (2) in Diagram 5-49). Against zones, (1) then screens away for (3), as (2) looks inside for (4) posting up.

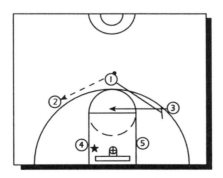

Diagram 5-49

(4) cuts to the corner, as (3) cuts to the middle of the zone.

(2) may then:

(A) pass to (3), who would shoot, look for (5) inside on a muscle post up or reverse the ball to (1). See Diagram 5-50.

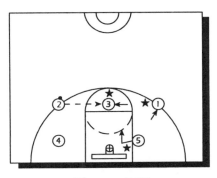

Diagram 5-50

(B) skip pass crosscourt to (1) for a possible three-point shot. See Diagram 5-51. Zones cannot cover (4)'s corner position and also cover a crosscourt pass to (1) behind the three-point line. If they spread out to attempt to cover the pass to (1), a pass to (3) can result in an easy shot for (5).

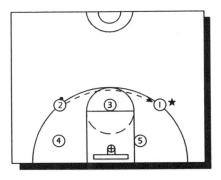

Diagram 5-51

(C) key the overload by passing to (4) in the corner. When this occurs, (1) replaces the point and (3) plays between the ball and the basket. See Diagram 5-52. The overload triangles are then utilized (see Diagram 5-53). When a change of sides is desired, (2) passes to (1) at the point and screens down for (4), who cuts to the wing, as (2) posts up. This move tells (3) to complete the loop maneuver by cutting around (5) to the offside wing. The ball is reversed to (3), as (5) screens the zone. See Diagram 5-54. (4) screens, steps up and posts up.

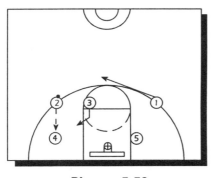

Diagram 5-52

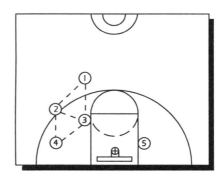

Diagram 5-53

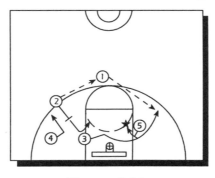

Diagram 5-54

As (1) reverses the ball, (1) must also look inside for (2) or (5) stepping up, who may be open if the zone becomes porous as it moves to cover this overshifted screen.

The same wing loop motion is then repeated on (3)'s side. The players must be made aware that too much motion is detrimental, and that each overload should be fully explored before a new change of sides.

The basic stack overload pattern plus the reset play and two pattern variations (quick lob and guard loop) spread out the defense by utilizing the deep ballside corner. This opens up the middle and allows some straight line cuts to the basket to be made. Covering the deep ballside corner is a new experience for many teams and forces them to make adjustments in their pressure and help defensive assignments. The fact that this player-to-player offense includes an overload makes it very adaptable versus zones.

This novel offensive approach is ideal if your opponent has a big player who dominates the lane area by blocking shots and rebounding. You can pull this player out of the lane and force him or her to cover the corner by initiating the offense on that side.

The stack overload pattern can also provide an excellent corner play variation for teams that run motion offenses, such as the shuffle, the passing game, or the flex.

CHAPTER 6

The Post Players Choice Offense

This two-phase offense starts from a 1-4 set. When necessary, it may be initiated from a double stack with big players (4) and (5) screening down for wings (2) and (3). The point (1) brings the ball into the front court and makes the entry pass. The motion is an interchangeable continuity because each of the five players will play every position as the pattern progresses. This makes it an ideal plan for teams without a dominant post player.

The Basic Offense

The two phases of this plan are keyed by the ballside post. Once the point passes to a wing and cuts through, the post will screen away. The ballside post can: (A) screen for the offside post directly across the lane, or (9) cut high to the offside high-post area and screen for the offside wing.

Phase I The Post to Post Screen

In Diagram 6-1, point (1) passes to wing (2) and cuts down the lane on the far side. Post (4) opts to screen away for (5), who cuts to the ballside post position. (3) moves down to screen for (1).

After screening for (5), (4) pops to the point. If (5) is not open, (2) passes to (4). If X5 is fronting (5), the pass to (4) changes the passing angle to (5) and he may be open after sealing X5 to receive a pass for a power lay-up shot. See Diagram 6-2.

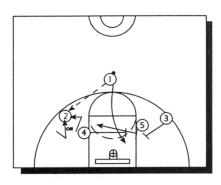

Post to Post Screen
Diagram 6-1

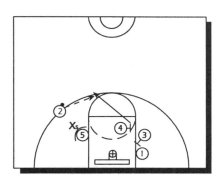

Pop to Point
Diagram 6-2

If (5) is not open, (4) may reverse the ball to (1) coming out of (3)'s downscreen to the wing area. See Diagram 6-3.

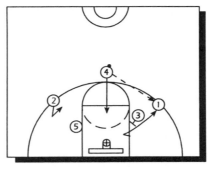

Pop Cut
Diagram 6-3

When this happens, the pattern may be repeated. See Diagrams 6-4 through 6-6.

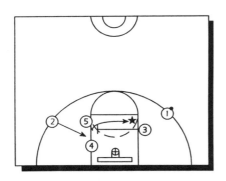

Post to Post Screen
Diagram 6-4

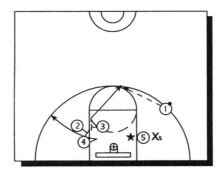

Pop to Point
Diagram 6-5

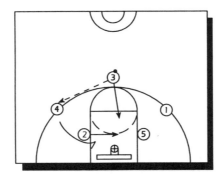

Pop Cut
Diagram 6-6

In the previous diagrams, when (3) receives the ball at the point, it is preferable that (3) reverse the ball to the opposite side. However, (3) could have returned the ball to (1) (who made a change of direction to get open) and run the pattern on that side. See Diagram 6-7.

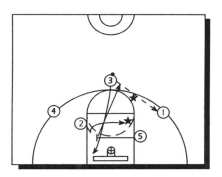

Post to Post Return Pass
Diagram 6-7

Phase II The Post-to-Wing Screen
This time after the point (1)'s pass to a wing (as to (2) in Diagram 6-8) and cut down the lane, the ballside post (4) chooses to key the post to offside wing screen. He or she does this by breaking to the offside high-post area.

The offside wing (3) fakes toward the baseline and then cuts over (4) to the ballside post area. See Diagram 6-9.

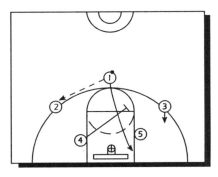

Post to Wing Screen
Diagram 6-8

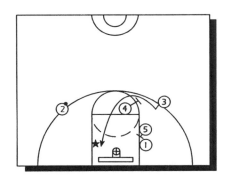

Diagram 6-9

After screening for (3), (4) cuts to the point. Then, if (3) is not open, (2) passes to (4), who reverses it to (1) coming out of (5)'s downscreen. The pattern is then repeated. See Diagrams 6-10 and 6-11.

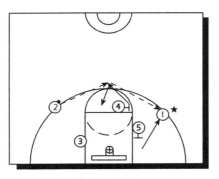

Pop to Point
Diagram 6-10

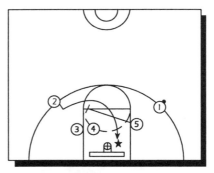

Post to Wing Screen
Diagram 6-11

The two patterns may be run interchangeably. After (4) reversed the ball to (1) in the previous diagrams, (5) could have screened away for (3) and called Phase 1, the Post-to-Post Screen Play. See Diagram 6-12.

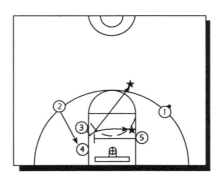

Post to Post Screen
Diagram 6-12

Coaching Note:
This offense often has no one at either guard position during a shot. It must be stressed that the offside wing is the safety who is responsible for the defensive balance when a shot is taken.

The Dribble Entry

The dribble-entry play for this offense is an integral part of the basic plan. It should be taught in the pre-season and used often.

Diagram 6-13 shows the point (1) unable to pass to a wing because of defensive denial. The player dribbles at and clears (2) across the lane. In effect, this dribble entry changes the assignments of (1) and (2).

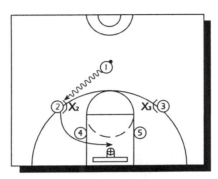

Dribble Entry Wing Clear
Diagram 6-13

The ballside post can then cut low and call the post to post screen (see Diagram 6-14), or cut high and key the post to wing screen. See Diagram 6-15.

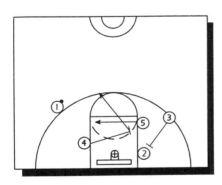

Diagram 6-14

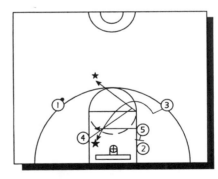

Post to Wing Screen
Diagram 6-15

This dribble entry may be used anytime the ball is at the point and the offense is in its original 1-4 set.

In most situations, the basic dribble entry play will suffice. However, if others are needed, the following will work.

The Wing Clear
When a wing is being denied the entry pass, the wing may clear out early across the lane and inform the ballside post by calling out "clear." This tells the post to move up to screen for the point. (1) then dribbles off the post and may shoot, or look for the post to: (A) roll to the basket, or (B) pop to the point.

(A) The Screen and Roll
When (4) uses the screen and roll in Diagram 6-16, the offside wing (3) hesitates and then takes the point. Then if neither (1) nor (4) is open, the ball may be reversed via (3). If (1) penetrates to a deep position, (3) must come to get the ball and dribble to the point before passing to (2). (2) must stay stacked under (5) until (3) is in position, and then pop to the wing. See Diagram 6-17.

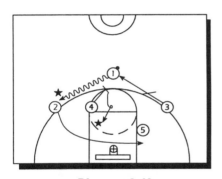
Diagram 6-16

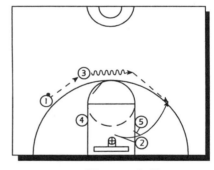
Diagram 6-17

Once the ball has been reversed to (2), (5) may key the basic offense by screening for (4) to key Phase I (see Diagram 6-18), or screening high and away for (1) to key Phase II (see Diagram 6-19).

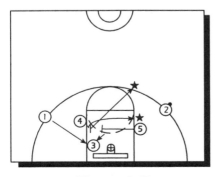
Diagram 6-18

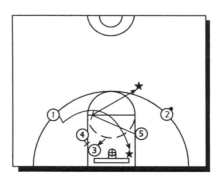
Diagram 6-19

(B) The Screen and Pop to the Point

This time, after screening for (1), (4) fakes the roll and pops to the point. If (4)'s defender is "hedging" on (1)'s dribble or involved in a switch, (4) may be open for a three-point shot. On the offside, (3) hesitates, fakes a cut to the point, and then cuts over (5) and (2). See Diagram 6-20.

(1) may then shoot, pass to (4), or look for (3) coming to the ballside low-post area off the double screen. Once the ball has been reversed to (2), the basic two-phase pattern is run with (5) keying one of the phases. See Diagram 6-21.

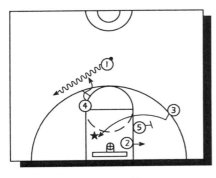

Screen and Pop
Diagram 6-20

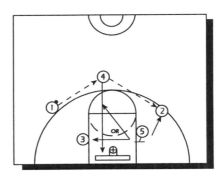

Diagram 6-21

The Backdoor Split

(2) is being denied the entry pass to start the basic two-phase pattern, so (4) breaks high and receives a bounce pass from (1). (2) backdoors X2 and if (2) does not get the ball, he or she stops at the lane. (1) follows the pass. See Diagram 6-22.

(1) comes down, screens for (2), and then rolls across the lane. (2) doubles back to the wing and receives the ball from (4). See Diagram 6-23.

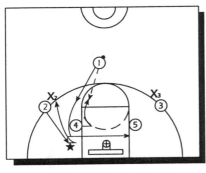

Wing Backdoor
Diagram 6-22

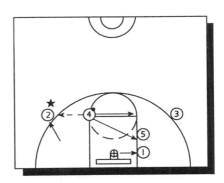

Backdoor Split
Diagram 6-23

(2)'s change of direction and the screen by (1) will very often result in a three-point shot for (2). If it does not, (4) cuts across the lane and may key either of the two phases.

Secondary Plays

The Screen-Screen Plays
(1) can key one of the screen-screen plays by passing to (2) and not cutting through.

Post-to-Post Screen-Screen
In Diagram 6-24, (1) passes to (2) and fakes a cut toward the ball as (4) screens away for (5). (5) cuts to the ballside and (4) pops high to screen for (1), who cuts to the offside lay-up area for a possible lob pass. See Diagram 6-25.

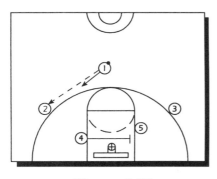
Diagram 6-24

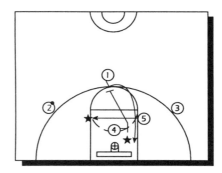
Diagram 6-25

If (5) and (1) are not open, (4) steps out, receives a pass back to (2), and reverses it to (1), coming out of (3)'s downscreen. See Diagram 6-26. Once (1) receives the ball, (3) can move across the lane and key either phase of the basic offense. See Diagram 6-27.

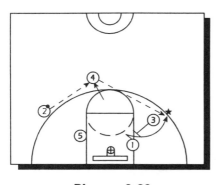
Diagram 6-26

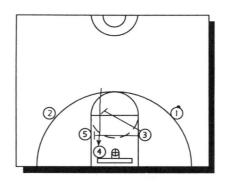
Diagram 6-27

The High-Post Screen-Screen

This time, when (1) passes to (2) and fakes in that direction, (4) opts to screen high for (3). (3) uses the screen to loop to the ballside and back to a position under (5). See Diagram 6-28.

(1) then slash cuts off (4) to the ballside post area. See Diagram 6-29.

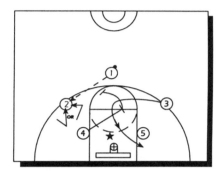

Diagram 6-28

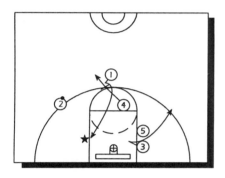

Diagram 6-29

If (1) is not open, (4) steps to the point, and the ball is reversed to (3), coming out of (5)'s downscreen. From there, (5) may call either of the two-phases by the cut and screen to the offside. See Diagram 6-30.

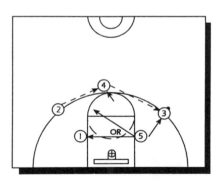

Diagram 6-30

The High Cut Plus the Mixer

The high cut phase of this offense works well when interjected into the mixer motion. Diagrams 6-31 and 6-32, show the mixer in progress.

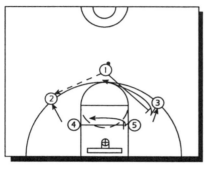

Mixer
Diagram 6-31

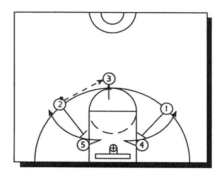

Diagram 6-32

As (5) receives the ball, (3) cuts down the middle instead of screening away for (4). This tells (2) to cut to the high post away from the ballside. (3) should call out "high" to alert (2), who may have his or her back turned to (3)'s cut. See Diagram 6-33.

(4) then cuts over (2) to the ballside low-post area, and (2) pops to the point. See Diagram 6-34.

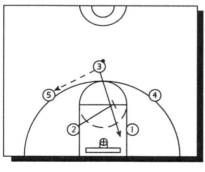

High Cut
Diagram 6-33

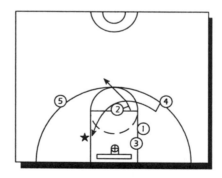

Point Pop
Diagram 6-34

(5) looks for (4), and then passes to (2) at the point. If (2) has no shot, (3) loops around (1)'s downscreen, as (5) screens down for (4). This puts the team back in the mixer pattern. See Diagrams 6-35 and 6-36.

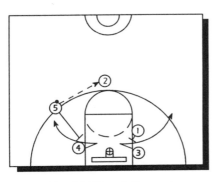

Double Stack Popout
Diagram 6-35

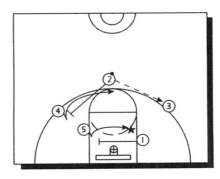

Mixer
Diagram 6-36

Phase III The Quick Shot Screen and Roll

A quick shot phase can be added by giving the ballside post a third screening possibility. In Diagram 6-37, (1) passes to (2), and again cuts down the middle. Previously, (4) had the two options shown in Diagram 6-37.

This time, (4) adds the quick shot option by stepping out to screen for (2). (2) dribbles off (4), and may shoot, hit (4) on the roll, or pass to (1), behind the double screen of (3) and (5). See Diagram 6-38.

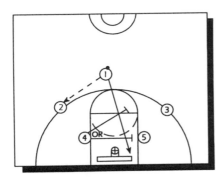

Diagram 6-37

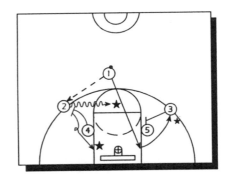

Diagram 6-38

If none of these options is open, (3) continues across the lane and loops around (4) to receive a pass from (2). See Diagram 6-39.

This pass to a wing restarts the now three-phase offense. See (4)'s options in Diagram 6-40.

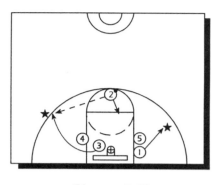

Diagram 6-39

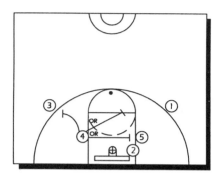

Diagram 6-40

The Shuffle Play

A shuffle play may be used as an option to the high-screen phase. Diagram 6-41 shows (1) passing to (2) and instead of cutting down the lane, (1) cuts at (3). This play variation tells (4) to screen high and (3) to cut low off (5) to the ballside low-post area. If X3 is cheating to get over the expected screen of (4), (3) may get an easy lay-up shot.

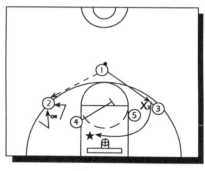

Diagram 6-41

If (3) is not open, (4) screens down for (5), who cuts to the point and then (4) rolls to the offside low post for a possible lob pass. See Diagram 6-42.

In most cases, (2) passes to (5) at the point, and the basic offense is run. See Diagram 6-43.

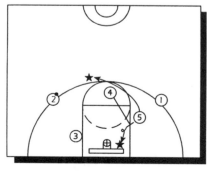

Diagram 6-42

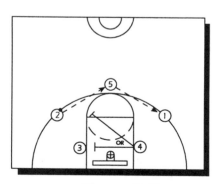

Diagram 6-43

Zone Potential

This offense can be adapted to be used against zone defenses. The result is a plan that tests the zone's middle, overloads it, and screens the overshift.

The High Screen to Overshift

Diagram 6-44 shows (1) passing to (2), and making the cut down the middle. (4), the ballside post, cuts to the offside high post, and (3) cuts to the middle of the zone.

If (2) can get the ball to (3), (3) can catch and face/turn and shoot, pass inside to (5) on a muscle post up, or reverse it to (1) at the offside wing. See Diagram 6-45.

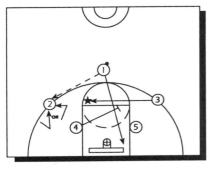

Diagram 6-44

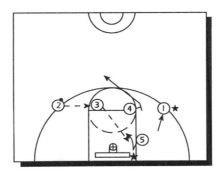

Diagram 6-45

If (2) cannot get the ball to (3), (2) passes to (4) at the point, who quickly reverses it to (1) who pops out of (5)'s screen of the zone. (3) drops low to rebound. See Diagram 6-46.

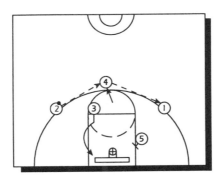

Overshift
Diagram 6-46

The High Screen to Overload

When (1) passes to (2) and cuts down the middle versus zones, (1) may also cut to the ballside corner. (4) breaks up and (3) cuts to the middle, and then to the ballside. These cuts overload (2)'s side of the court. See Diagram 6-47.

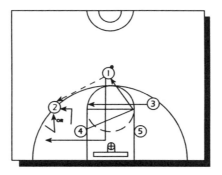

Diagram 6-47

(2) may then: (A) pass to (3) who can shoot or look inside for (5) on a muscle post up (see Diagram 6-48) or (B) utilize the overload triangles (see Diagram 6-49).

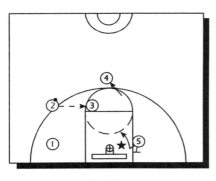

Overload
Diagram 6-48

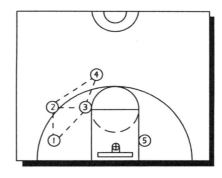

Diagram 6-49

The overload is maintained until the initial cutter (1) decides to cancel it. Player (1) does this by cutting across the lane and around (5)'s screen of the zone players. The ball is reversed to (1). Once the offense is balanced, the new point (4) will cut through and key an overload or overshift play by the direction of the cut. See Diagrams 6-50 and 6-51.

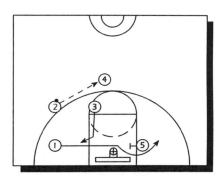

Switch Sides
Diagram 6-50

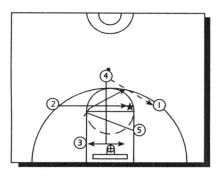

Diagram 6-51

The post's choice offense is an ideal plan for teams lacking a dominant big player. It uses the ballside post to key which of its two basic phases will be run. Teams may also blend one or both of its phases with other patterns, such as the passing game mixer or the shuffle.

CHAPTER 7

The UCLA Passing Game

This chapter demonstrates how the UCLA slash and downscreen play may be used as an adjunct to the passing game. Combining this quick-hitting play with a motion game permits a team to get a quick shot, or to run some time off the clock before shooting. The result is an all-purpose offense that is adaptable to the tempo demands made necessary by the shot clock, and the makeable three point shot.

This offense is best suited for a team with one big pivot player (5) and four mobile perimeter players.

The Basic Offense

Diagram 1-1 shows (1) passing to the ballside forward (3) and joining the high post (5) in a double screen for (4). (2) uses (1) and (5) to make a UCLA slash cut to the ballside low-post area and (4) cuts to the point.

If (2) is not open, (2) clears halfway to the ballside corner (short corner), and (5) uses (1) to cut back to the ballside post. See Diagram 7-2.

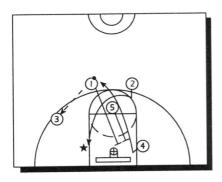

Slash Double
Diagram 7-1

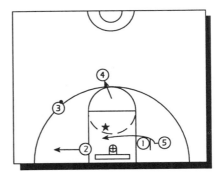

Corner Clear
Diagram 7-2

If (3) passes to (5), he or she makes a one-on-one pivot play. In Diagram 7-3 , (3) passes to (4) at the point. This pass is followed by (3)'s downscreen for (2) (ala UCLA), and (1)'s cut to the offside wing position for a possible three-point shot if the defense is sagging.

(4) may then: (A) pass to (2) and screen away for (1). (Also note that after screening, (3) moves to the other side of the lane.) See Diagram 7-4.

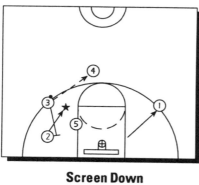

Screen Down
Diagram 7-3

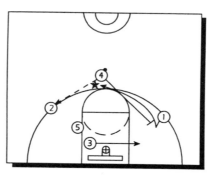

Reset
Diagram 7-4

Last Shot Special
When running this option and seeking a quick shot, (5) may join (3) in the downscreen for (2). See Diagram 7-5.

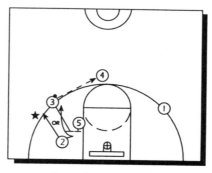

Last Shot Double
Diagram 7-5

(B) (4)'s second option after receiving the ball from (3) is to pass to (1) and cut away, as per the passing game. (4) may simply screen away for (2) (see Diagram 7-6) or receive a screen from (2) that allows him or her to cut to the offside lay-up area for a possible lob pass. This pass is made possible because (3) cleared across the lane after screening and (5) always swings to the ballside mid-post area. See Diagram 7-7.

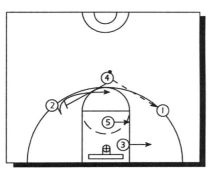

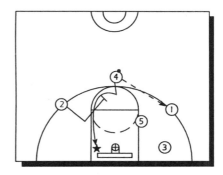

Last Shot Single
Diagram 7-6

Last Shot Lob
Diagram 7-7

Note that (2) pinched in as (4) passed to (1) to create a proper screening angle on (4)'s defender.

Whichever option is run, (2) ends up at the point. (1) can then pass to (2) and downscreen for (3). This pass tells (4) to clear to the wing area to provide a three-point option and make it more difficult for X4 to help in the lane. See Diagram 7-8.

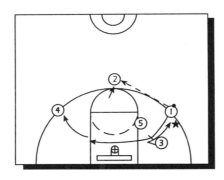

Diagram 7-8

From there, the same options may be run. (2) may: (A) pass to (3) and screen away for (4); or (B) pass to (4) and cut away to set a screen, or to receive a screen for a lob pass. The UCLA downscreener always clears across the lane and the post (5) always swings to the ballside.

The Dribble Entry

When a guard cannot make the initial entry pass, the guard may resort to a dribble entry. Diagram 7-9 shows (3) being denied the pass from (1). Seeing this, (1) dribbles at (3), who cuts toward the lane and then to a position half-way to the corner (short corner). (2), the offside guard, then cuts over (5), looking for a pass from (1). If this pass is not thrown, (2) clears across the lane to a position below (4).

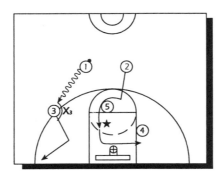

Dribble Entry Passing Game
Diagram 7-9

(5) then screens for (4), who cuts to the point. After screening, (5) rolls back to the ballside of the lane. See Diagram 7-10.

(1) can pass to (5) for a pivot shot, or to (4) and screen down for (3) to start the motion. (2) cuts to the three-point area. See Diagram 7-11.

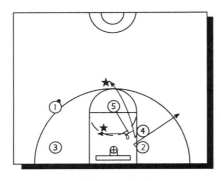

Diagram 7-10

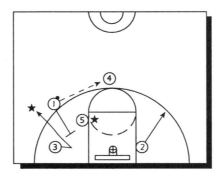

Diagram 7-11

Alternate Dribble Entry Play

Diagram 7-12 shows another dribble entry play that may be used when the entry pass is being denied. (1)'s *dribble clears* (3) across the lane. (2) hesitates until (3) clears the lane, and then makes a slash cut over or under (5) and to the ballside low-post area. If (2) is not open, (2) continues the cut to the short corner.

(5) then screens for (4), and then rolls to the ballside post area. See Diagram 7-13.

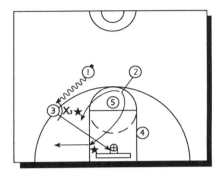

Dribble Entry Wing Clear
Diagram 7-12

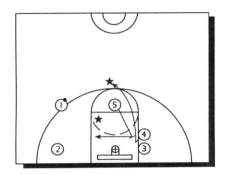

Diagram 7-13

From that set, the basic options may be run.

One of these dribble-entry plays should be taught in the pre-season to help relieve defensive pressure.

Secondary Plays

As the season progresses, it may become necessary to add depth to the offense. At that time, the fake slash play, the corner lob play, or the "you come, I come" play may be added. This should be done only when the need becomes very obvious.

The Fake Slash Entry

This play is a variation of the UCLA slash play that initiates the basic offense. Diagram 7-14 shows (1) passing to the ballside forward (3) and joining (5) to double screen for (4). This time, however, (2) fakes the cut under (5) and doubles back to the point. Seeing (2)'s move, (4) cuts across the lane off the double screen. See Diagram 7-15.

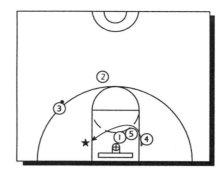

Slash Double Wing Pop
Diagram 7-14

Diagram 7-15

If (4) is not open, (4) clears half-way to the short corner and then (5) uses (1) to cut to the ballside mid-post area. See Diagram 7-16.

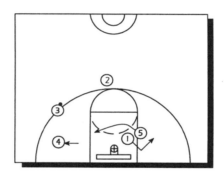

Corner Clear—Post Across
Diagram 7-16

From there, to continue the motion, (3) will pass to (2), and the basic options will prevail with (2) and (4) exchanging assignments. This play works well to obtain a quick three-point shot for (2).

The Corner Lob Play

Diagram 7-17 shows that the strongside wing (3) has the ball, and a pass to either (4) or (5) is being denied. (3) keys the corner lob play by passing to (2) in the corner and cutting over post (5) for a possible lob or bounce pass. (5) then rolls to the basket. (5) may be open if the defender X5 stepped out to hedge on (3)'s cut .

If neither (3) nor (5) is open, (2) dribbles to the wing, (3) clears half-way to the offside corner, and (4) screens away for (1). (4)'s screen is important because (1) must come to help if (2) is trapped in the corner. See Diagram 7-18.

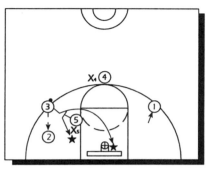

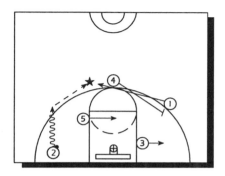

Corner Lob
Diagram 7-17

Diagram 7-18

Once (1) receives the ball and it is reversed to (4), the basic options will be available. See Diagram 7-19.

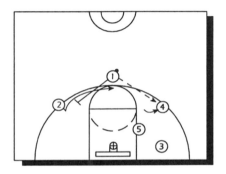

Diagram 7-19

The You Come, I Come Play

If post (5) is an adept passer, this play will be an excellent addition. (5) always swings to the ballside. If the strongside wing will pass to him or her, one of two options may be run. (A) (3) may screen for (2) and roll to the basket as (4) backdoors the defender. See Diagram 7-20.

Or (B) (3) may screen for (4) and roll to the basket as (2) backdoors the defender. See Diagram 7-21.

It is important for (1) to move to the wing position when a pass is made to (5). (2) becomes a three-point option if the defense collapses on (5), and also provides defensive balance by being the first person back as safety.

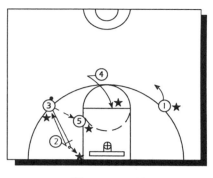

Diagram 7-20

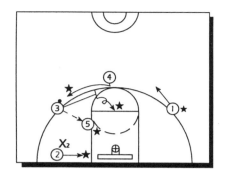

Diagram 7-21

Zone Potential

This offense may be adapted to run against zones by coaches who prefer an overload strategy. Diagram 7-22 shows the ball being passed around the four-player perimeter. This will usually establish an adjusting zone in a two-player front (2-3 or 2-1-2).

Once these passes have been made, (1) (or (2)) may initiate the motion by passing to the forward, and joining (5) to screen for the offside forward ((4) in Diagram 7-23) then cutting through directly to the ballside corner.

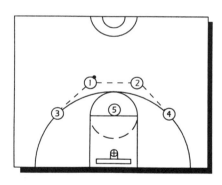

Two-Guard Front
Diagram 7-22

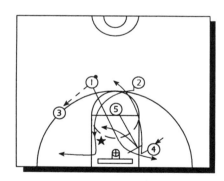

One-Guard Front
Diagram 7-23

(4) uses the double screen to cut to the point. The dual cut of (1) and (5) may impede the slides of the zone players.

Overload

This double screen usually has little effect on (4)'s getting open, but it gives (5)'s subsequent cut to the ballside a better angle. If (5) receives the ball, (5) can shoot or look for (1). Against zones, (1) is given more freedom. He or she may stay in the low post or move out to the wing. Either of these positions puts (1) in a good place to receive a pass from (5). If (1) stays inside, he or she may receive a pass for a power lay-up shot or a muscle post up. See Diagram 7-24. If (1) moves out to the wing and the zone has collapsed on (5), he or she may be open for a three-point shot. See Diagram 7-25.

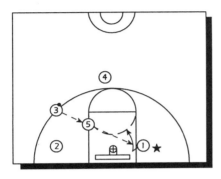

Diagram 7-24

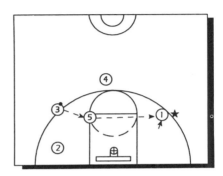

Diagram 7-25

Changing the Overload

If a pass is not made to (5) on the post up cut to the ball, it is moved around the overload triangles with no passing game player movement until the strongside wing (3) decides to switch the overload. (3) does this by passing to (4) at the point and screening the zone to allow corner player (2) to move to the wing. See Diagram 7-26. Player (3) then continues across the lane and toward the opposite corner. (4) attempts to help (2) get open by faking in the opposite direction and even taking a dribble that way. (4) then passes back to (2) if he or she is open. (1) moves to the wing position.

If (2) is not open, (3) continues to the corner, (5) swings to the ballside, and the same overload options are available once (4) passes to (1). See Diagram 7-27.

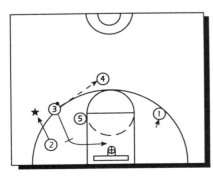

Diagram 7-26

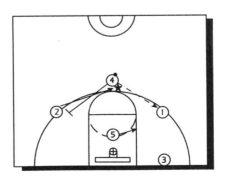

Diagram 7-27

(1) is now the strongside wing, who will switch the overload if necessary. The players must be taught that too much player movement versus zones is not effective. The ball should be passed around the overload triangles to really test the zone. Explore the areas and gaps before moving.

Having a forward at the point as in the previous examples has both positive and negative effects. The forward is taller than most point players to be able to see over small front zone players and, at times, get the ball inside to (5). However, the point must be the first player back on defense, and this negates his or her ability to rebound unless this safety assignment is switched with another designated player.

The zone phase of this offense has a changing perimeter, overloads, screens the overload, and attempts to get the ball inside.

This UCLA passing game offense has the quick-shot potential in its passing game component. It also may be used against zones. These attributes make it a good all-purpose offense.

CHAPTER 8

The Inside Triangle Offense

The inside triangle offense provides many basic scoring options within the context of motion. It is an inside-oriented plan that may be run in many ways. Here are two of them:

Method I Screen Away and Screen Down

The most popular method of running the inside triangle offense from a 1-2-2 set starts from a double stack. Diagram 8-1 shows (2) and (3) popping out of the downscreens of their respective big players ((4) and (5)). (1) passes to (2) and this keys the ballside post (4) to screen away for (5), who cuts to the ballside post area.

(1) then comes down and screens for (4), who pops to the point. If (5) is not open, (2) passes to (4). See Diagram 8-2.

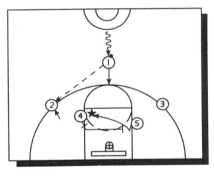

Screen Away
Diagram 8-1

Screen Down
Diagram 8-2

If (5) had been fronted, (4) may now be able to pass to (5) for a power lay-up. However, in most cases, (4) reverses the ball to (1) coming out of (3)'s downscreen. See Diagram 8-3.

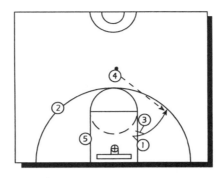

Diagram 8-3

(3) then screens across the lane for (5) and the pattern is repeated. See Diagrams 8-4 and 8-5.

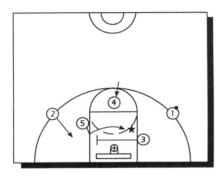

Screen Across
Diagram 8-4

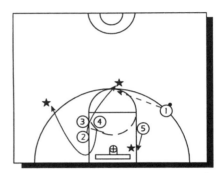

Screen Down
Diagram 8-5

The UCLA Entry

This same pattern may be initiated via the UCLA downscreen play. Diagram 8-6 shows (1) passing to wing (2), and slashing off (4), who stepped up to the high-post area. After screening, (4) moves to the point and receives a pass from (2), who then screens down for (1). (1) pops to the wing. See Diagram 8-7.

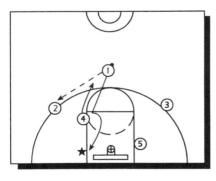

Slash Cut
Diagram 8-6

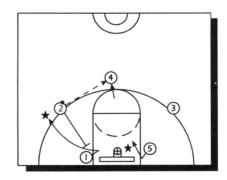

Pop Cut
Diagram 8-7

(4) passes to (1), and (2) moves across the lane to screen for (5). (4) then downscreens for (2), who cuts to the point. See Diagrams 8-8 and 8-9.

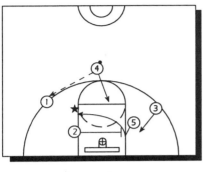

Screen Across
Diagram 8-8

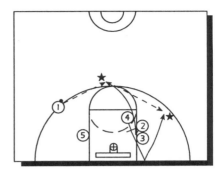

Screen Down
Diagram 8-9

The UCLA downscreen play can also be initiated after the shot clock has been run down to an appropriate time.

Pressure Relievers

The Dribble-Entry Lob
When there is defensive pressure on the perimeter, the dribble-entry lob may be keyed. Diagram 8-10 shows (1) dribbling at (2), and clearing (2) across the lane to the offside wing that was vacated by (3), who cut to the point. (1) passes to (3).

(3) passes to (2), and cuts off a screen by (4) to the offside lay-up area for a possible lob pass. (3) must wait until (4) stops and assumes a back screening stance and position before making the cut. See Diagram 8-11.

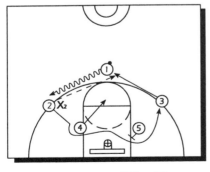

Dribble Entry—Wing Clear
Diagram 8-10

Point Lob
Diagram 8-11

If (3) is not open, (5) screens for (4), who cuts to the ballside low post. After screening, (5) pops to the point. See Diagram 8-12.

If (4) is not open, (2) passes to (5), and the ball is reversed to (3) coming out of (1)'s downscreen. See Diagram 8-13.

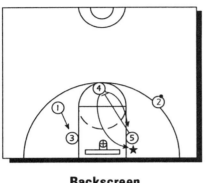

Backscreen
Diagram 8-12

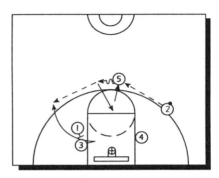

Pop Cut
Diagram 8-13

From there, (1) screens away for (4) and the basic screen away and screen down pattern is resumed. See Diagram 8-14.

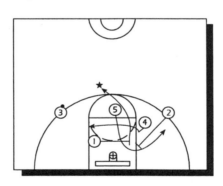

Triangle
Diagram 8-14

These three plays (the basic pattern, UCLA entry play, and the dribble-entry lob) constitute the basic offensive plan of Method I.

Method II The Downscreener Calls the Play

This method starts in the same manner with (1) passing to a wing (as to (2) in Diagram 8-15) who came out of a downscreen by (4). On the far side, (3) came out of (5)'s downscreen.

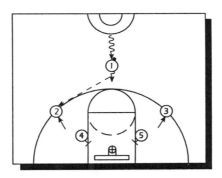

Diagram 8-15

At this juncture, (4), the ballside post, is the key player The ballside post's options are: (A) to screen away for (5), or (B) to screen high for (1).

(A) The screen away for (5) is the basic play that was previously mentioned. (4) screens away for (5) (see Diagram 8-16) and then (1) screens down for 4 (see Diagram 8-17).

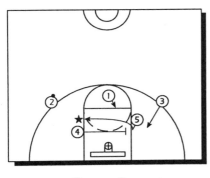

**Screen Away
Diagram 8-16**

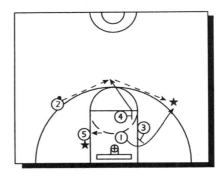

Diagram 8-17

(B) When (4) opts to screen high for (1), (4) loops to the ballside low-post area. See Diagram 8-18.

(5) then moves up and screens for (4), who cuts to the offside lay-up area for a possible lob pass. See Diagram 3-19.

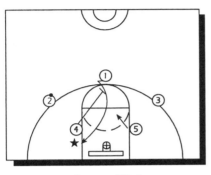 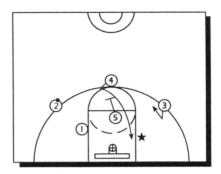

Screen High
Diagram 8-18

Screen Up-Lob
Diagram 8-19

If neither (1) nor (4) was open, (2) passes to (5), who popped to the point after screening for (4). See Diagram 8-20.

(3) must wait until (5) receives the ball before screening down for (4). Otherwise, (3)'s defender X3 will jam up the possible lob pass to (4). See Diagram 8-21.

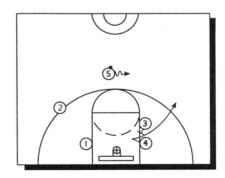

Diagram 8-20

Pop Cut
Diagram 8-21

In Diagram 8-21, (3) is now the player who will determine the type of triangle pattern to be run by screening away for (1), or high for (5). Following (3)'s screen, the third member of the triangle will screen for the screener (3).

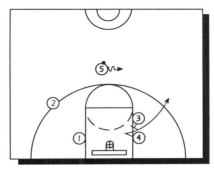

Diagram 8-21

The UCLA Entry

Method II may also be initiated via the UCLA slash and downscreen play. Diagram 8-22 shows (1) pass to (2) and slash off (4), who moved up to set the screen. (2) then passes to (4), who popped to the head of the key, and downscreens to allow (1) to cut to the wing. See Diagram 8-23.

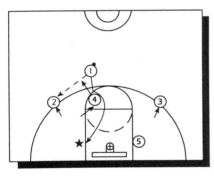

Slash Cut
Diagram 8-22

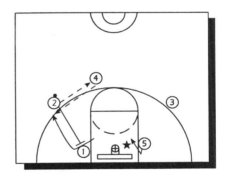

Pop Cut
Diagram 8-23

(2) is now the key player, who will call the type of inside triangle play to be run via the screen away for (5), or screen high for (4). See Diagram 8-24.

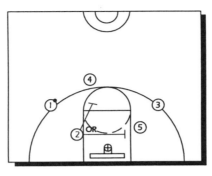

Diagram 8-24

Pressure Reliever

The Dribble Entry Play

A dribble entry play may also be used to initiate Method II of the inside triangle play. Diagram 8-25 shows (1) dribble at (2), and clear him or her across the lane to receive (5)'s downscreen. (1) stops at the wing and passes to (3), who replaced (1) at the point.

(3) looks first for (4), who was fronted when (1) had the ball at the wing. Once (2) receives the ball on the reversal, (5) becomes the key player who will call the type of triangle pattern to be run by screening away for (4), or high for (5). The third member of the triangle will then screen the screener. See Diagram 8-26.

Dribble Entry—Wing Clear
Diagram 8-25

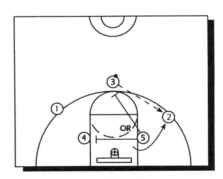

Triangle
Diagram 8-26

The basic inside triangle play, the UCLA entry, and the dribble-entry play are the core of both methods of running this offense. They should be ready at the beginning of the season.

Secondary Plays

These secondary plays may be used with either method. They should be added only when and if needed.

The Outside Cut Lob Play

(1) keys this play by passing to a wing (as to (2) in Diagram 8-27) and making an outside cut. This tells the offside post (5) to break to the ballside high-post area. (2) returns the ball to (1) on a handoff pass and cuts over (5) to the offside lay-up area for a possible lob pass.

If (2) is not open, (5) pops to the point and receives a pass from (1). Player (5) then reverses the ball to (2), coming out of (3)'s downscreen. See Diagram 8-28.

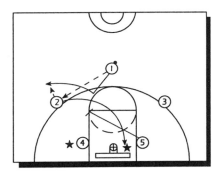

Outside Cut Lob
Diagram 8-27

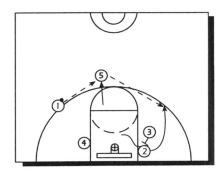

Diagram 8-28

At this point, a coach has three possible play options. The coach may:

(A) Treat the outside-cut lob play like the dribble-entry lob. See Diagram 8-29.

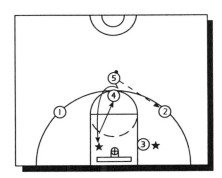

Point Lob
Diagram 8-29

(8) Use Method I, which is a screen away followed by a screen down. See Diagram 8-30.

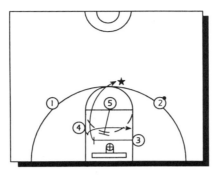

Screen Away
Diagram 8-30

(C) Use Method II and allow downscreener (3) to choose the type of triangle rotation to be run. See Diagram 8-31.

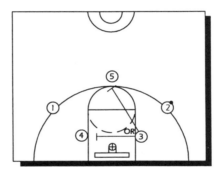

Screen Away or High
Diagram 8-31

The Shuffle Entry

The shuffle entry to the inside triangle offense gives it many more scoring options. It is keyed when the ballside post man ((4) in Diagram 8-32) moves up to a high-post position. Then when (1) passes to (2), the offside wing (3) cuts off post (5) and moves to the ballside low-post area.

After (3) cuts, (5) moves up and back-screens (1)'s defender to allow (1) to cut to the offside lay-up area for a possible lob pass. See Diagram 8-33.

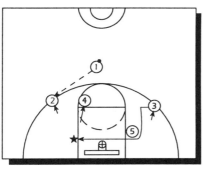

Diagram 8-32

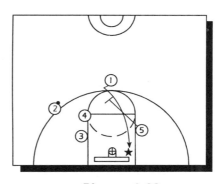

Diagram 8-33

If (1) is not open, (5) steps to the point, receives a pass from (2), and reverses it to (1), cutting to the wing. (2) then cuts low and to the ballside of the double screen of (4) and (3). See Diagram 8-34.

(5) and (4) move down to screen for (3), who cuts to the point. If (2) was not open, (1) passes to (3) at the point. See Diagram 8-35.

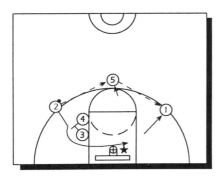

Diagram 8-34

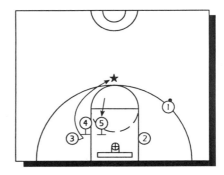

Diagram 8-35

(1) then screens down for (2) as (5) loops around (4). (3) can then pass to either side (as to (5) in Diagram 8-36). This pass will start the inside triangle motion.

Diagram 8-36

Method I can be run with (4) screening across for (1) and (3) screening down for (4). See Diagram 8-37. Method II can be keyed with (4) screening for either (1) or (3). See Diagram 8-38. The third member of the triangle will then screen the screener.

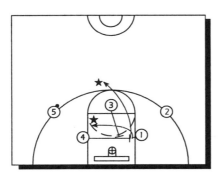

Screen Away
Diagram 8-37

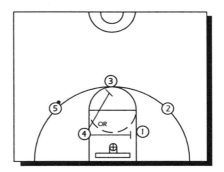

Screen Away or High
Diagram 8-38

A Two-Player Front Entry
When a team lacks a point guard who can handle defensive pressure, they can initiate the triangle offense from a two-player front.

Diagram 8-39 shows guards (1) and (2) bringing the ball into the front court. (1) passes to (2) and cuts down the center of the lane. Player (1) may then: (A) cut around (4), or (B) around (5) and (3).

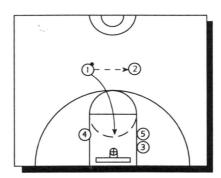

Single Double
Diagram 8-39

(A) The Cut Around (4)

When (1) cuts around the single downscreen of (4), it tells (3), who was stacked under (5), to pop to the other wing. See Diagram 3-40.

(2) may then pass to a wing and initiate the desired method of running the inside triangle offense. Diagram 8-41, shows (2) passing to (1) and the ballside post (4) having the choices of screening across or high that are associated with Method II.

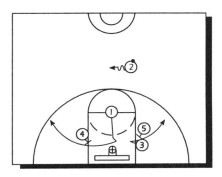

Single Side
Diagram 8-40

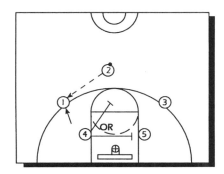

Screen Away or High
Diagram 8-41

(B) The Cut Around (5) and (3)

When (1) passed to (2), and cut down the lane, (4) could have cut around the stack formed by (5) and (3). See Diagram 8-42.

This cut by (1) tells (3) to move across the lane because (3) always cuts to the wing opposite (1). He or she uses the downscreen of (4) to get open. See Diagram 8-43.

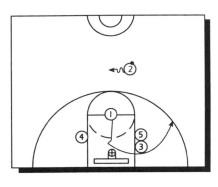

Double Side
Diagram 8-42

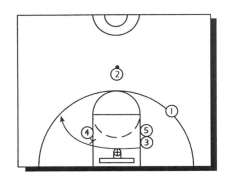

Diagram 8-43

(2) then passes to either wing and the onside post initiates the desired method of running the inside triangle offense.

The Wing Slash Play

The wing slash play is a quick hitter that may be run as the inside triangle motion is in progress. Diagram 8-44 shows the post (4) breaking up and receiving a bounce pass from (1) then catching and facing the basket. (1) then breaks to the opposite wing. This key tells the offside wing (3) to slash off (5) to the ballside post area.

If (3) is not open, (5) muscle posts. (5) is taught to force a switch between (5)'s defender X5 and X3, and then trap X3 outside him or her as (5) turns toward the basket. See Diagram 8-45.

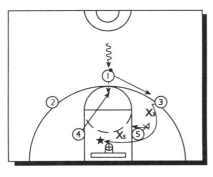

Wing Slash
Diagram 8-44

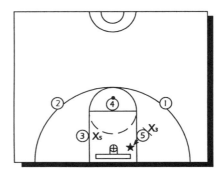

Diagram 8-45

If neither (3) nor (5) is open, (4) can pass to either wing and restart the inside triangle motion. Usually (2) and (1) must fake toward the baseline and then come back to the ball in order to get open. Diagram 8-46 shows (5) starting Method I and Diagram 8-47 shows him or her starting Method II.

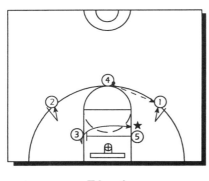

Triangle
Diagram 8-46

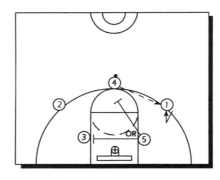

Triangle
Diagram 8-47

However, in most cases, a shot will be taken before the offense must be reset.

Since the offside screens of the triangle offense have little effect on zone defenses, an adapted version is run. This method starts from a stack that attempts to trap the zone inside, tests the zone's middle with a triangle play, and then screens the ball reversal. An overload play is keyed via a dribble entry to give the offense more depth.

The Zone Motion Triangle Play

(A) The Stack Phase

Diagram 8-48 shows big players (4) and (5) downscreening for (2) and (3) in order to trap the zone inside. (1) may then pass to either wing, or throw directly to one of the big players inside the zone.

This move forces the zone to cover both wings without becoming too porous inside. This is a difficult assignment.

In most cases, the ball is passed to a wing (as to (2) in Diagram 8-49). When this happens, the point (1) slides to the three-point area away from the ball, and the offside post (5) breaks to the high post. (3), the offside wing, replaces (5) in the offside low-post area.

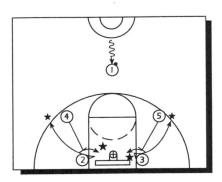

Double Stack Popout
Diagram 8-48

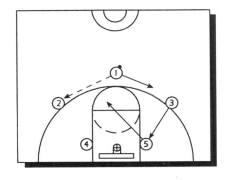

Triangle
Diagram 8-49

(B) Triangle Phase

(2) may then: pass to (5) in the middle of the zone, or pass to (1) for a three-point shot. When (5) receives the ball, the triangle play is run. (5) may turn, square up and shoot, or drop the ball inside to (4) or (3). See Diagram 8-50.

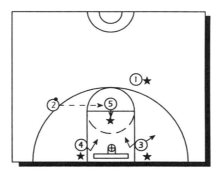

Diagram 8-50

(C) The Screened Reversal Phase

If (5) is not open inside the zone, (5) pops to the point. This tells (1) to cut to the ballside low post after (4) clears across the lane and around (3)'s downscreen of the zone. See Diagrams 8-51 and 8-52.

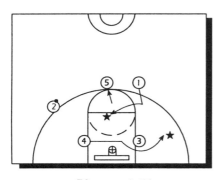

Diagram 8-51

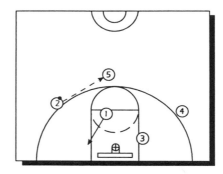

Diagram 8-52

(D) The Start Over Phase

After passing to (5), (2) screens down for (1). This downscreen plus (4)'s cut around (3) amount to a double stack, and (5) may pass to either wing or directly inside to one of the screeners. The zone is again trapped inside and a pass to a wing (as to (4) in Diagram 8-53) initiates a new play sequence. See Diagram 8-54.

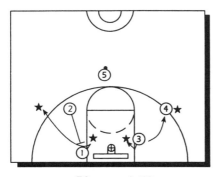

Diagram 8-53

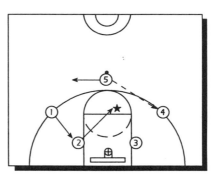

Diagram 8-54

Cross Court Pass Play

(A) The Three-Point Phase

When the stack opens up (as in Diagram 8-49) and the cross court pass to the former point ((1) in Diagram 8-55) is made, (1) should be in the three-point area and prepared to shoot. When the pass is made and (1) cannot shoot, he or she looks first for (4), looping around (3), and then for (5), stepping to the point.

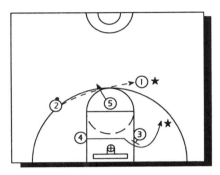

Diagram 8-55

(B) The Start Over Phase

After (1) passes to either (4) or (5), he or she cuts down and around the downscreen of (2), and a new play sequence may be run. See Diagrams 8-56 and 8-57.

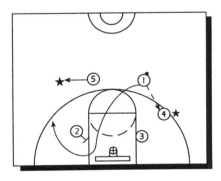

Diagram 8-56

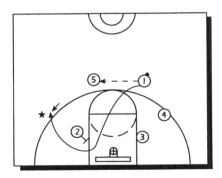

Diagram 8-57

The Dribble-Entry Play

The dribble entry may be used to (A) initiate the basic offense, or (B) to create an overload.

(A) Initiating the Offense

Diagram 8-58 shows (1) dribbling at (2) and clearing him or her across the lane. The ball is then reversed to (2) by (3), who took the point. (3) cuts away from the pass to the three-point area and (4) breaks high. This starts the basic zone motion. See Diagram 8-59.

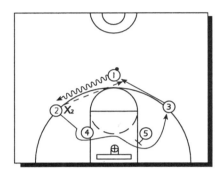

Dribble Entry—Wing Clear
Diagram 8-58

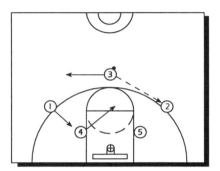

Diagram 8-59

(B) Creating an Overload

In Diagram 8-60, (1) again dribbles at (2). This time, however, (2) creates an overload by cutting to the ballside corner in a corner push moves.

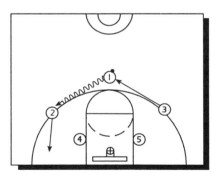

Dribble Entry—Corner Push
Diagram 8-60

The overload triangles are then utilized until (2) decides to initiate the basic zone motion. (2) does this by cutting across the lane and around (5). The ball is then reversed to (2) via (3) as (4) cuts high and (3) slides away from the pass to the three-point area. See Diagrams 8-61 and 8-62.

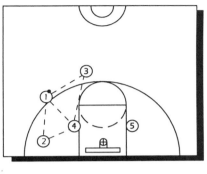

Overload
Diagram 8-61

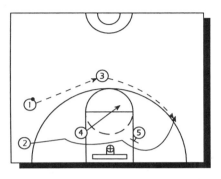

Switch Sides
Diagram 8-62

This zone offense has three-point potential, a changing perimeter, checks the zone's middle, screens the overshift, and tests the corner via an overload.

The triangle offense moves the defense and attempts to get the ball inside. Much attention must be devoted to getting the ball from the wing to the ballside post. The offside wing is the back safety, and the rebounding triangle is built in. This offense is a five-player continuity. When your team has a strong big post, the other players should not screen down for him or her when that post is the offside post and they are in the offside wing position. This keeps the big player inside and in the triangle motion.

The continuity motion of this plan allows a team to kill the clock and then get a good shot. The basic plays that are included (stack, UCLA, dribble entry, etc.) allow them to get a quick shot when the time-score constraints demand it.

CHAPTER 9

The Box and One Dribble-Entry Offense

This chapter covers the box and one dribble-entry offense and its three functions. It may be used as: a primary offense by up-tempo teams with physical players, a quick-shot alternative in short time situations, or as a "closer" after a team has run the shot or game clock down to a pre-designated point and wants to get a high-percentage shot. This offense is designed to be run against pressure and help player-to-player defenses, but it may be adapted to be used versus zones.

The Basic Box and One Dribble-Entry Offense

Following are six plays that utilize this formation. A coach should find the two or three that best fit the skills of the coach's personnel and work out play keys to differentiate between them. These signals could be (A) oral or hand keys; (B) determined by the specific location of the personnel within the box (i.e. big players on top or small players on top); or by the direction the point (1) makes the dribble entry (i.e. a dribble to the right calls one play and to the left another). The signals must then become automatic through repetitive practice.

I. The Double Down Play

Diagram 9-1 shows (1) bringing the ball into the front court and the box formed in this case with big players ((4) and (5)) at the top, and smaller players ((2) and (3)) at the bottom.

(1) may dribble off either post (as off (4) in Diagram 9-1). This tells (2) to screen away for (3), who cuts to the ballside.

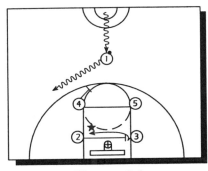

Diagram 9-1

(4) and (5) then double down for good shooter (2), who pops to the three-point area. See Diagram 9-2.

If (3) is not open, (1) passes to (2). This pass tells (4) to loop around (5) to the open wing and become the third option. See Diagram 9-3.

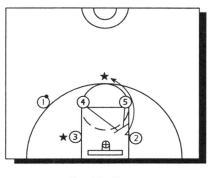

Double Down
Diagram 9-2

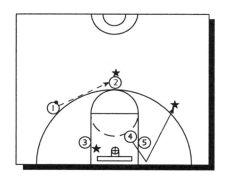

Diagram 9-3

The team is now back in its basic 1-2-2 pattern set.

II. The Loop Play
This time after (1) makes the dribble entry, the offside low post ((3) in Diagram 9-4) fakes a cut off (2)'s screen and cuts to the point. (4) and (5) stay high, but attempt to form a double screen.

If (3) is not open, (3) continues to loop to the ballside low-post area that was vacated by (2) who crossed the lane. (4) and (5) then come down to screen for (2), who cuts to the three-point area at the point. See Diagram 9-5.

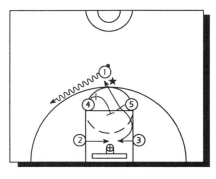

Double Down
Diagram 9-4

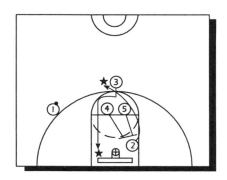

Loop Down
Diagram 9-5

If (3) is not open at the point or in the low-post area, (1) passes to (2) at the point for a possible three pointer. If this shot is not open, (4) loops around (5) to the offside wing, and the team is in its basic 1-2-2 set. See Diagram 9-6.

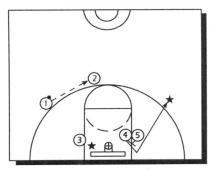

Diagram 9-6

III. The Double-Double Play
This time, (1) dribbles off high post (5) and to a wing position. Both players on the ballside of the box screen away for (4), who cuts diagonally to the ballside low-post area. See Diagram 9-7.

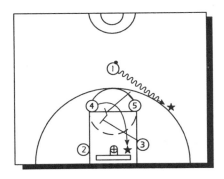

Diagram 9-7

(3) and (5) then roll down to screen for (2), who pops to the three-point area at the head of the key. If (4) is not open, (1) passes to (2) and screens down for (4), who cuts to the wing. (3) uses (5) to cut to the opposite wing. See Diagrams 9-8 and 9-9.

(2) may shoot for three or initiate the basic offense from a 1-2-2 set.

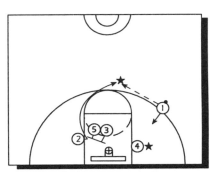

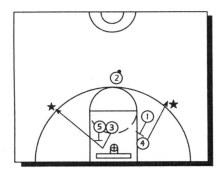

Double Down
Diagram 9-8

Double Stack Popout
Diagram 9-9

IV. The X Play

(1) dribbles to a wing. This tells (2), the ballside low post in Diagram 9-10, to move diagonally across the lane and screen for (5), who cuts to the ballside low post. (2) rolls to the far wing for a possible three-point shot.

If (5) is not open, (4) completes the X by screening down for (3), who cuts to the three-point area at the head of the key. See Diagram 9-11.

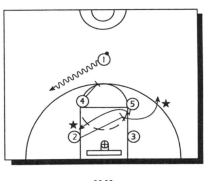

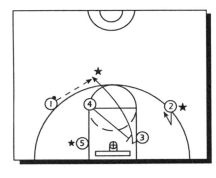

X Up
Diagram 9-10

X Down
Diagram 9-11

Once (3) receives the ball, (3) may shoot, or key a play from the 1-2-2 set.

V. The Box Shuffle

(1) dribbles off high post (4) as the low post on side (2) clears to the ballside corner to allow (4) to roll to the basket on the ball side of the lane. (5) screens down for (3), who pops to the point. See Diagram 9-12.

If (4) is not open on the roll, (1) passes to (3), who can shoot for three points, or reverse the ball to (5), who moved out to the wing position. (2) then cuts off (4) to the ballside low-post area. See Diagram 9-13.

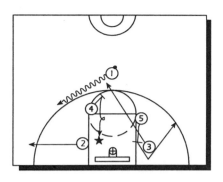

Diagram 9-12

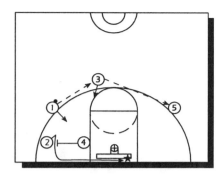

Baseline Shuffle
Diagram 9-13

If (2) is not open, (1) and (3) screen down for (4), who cuts to the three-point area at the point. See Diagram 9-14.

When (5) passes to (4), (5) downscreens for (2) as (3) loops around (1) on the other side. From there, a 1-2-2 play sequence may be run. See Diagram 9-15.

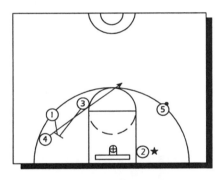

Double Down
Diagram 9-14

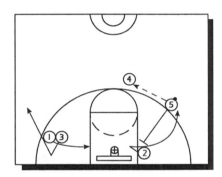

Double Stack Popout
Diagram 9-15

V. The Roll or Pop Play

As (1) dribbles off high post (4), the ballside post (2) clears across the lane. (4) may then: (A) roll to the basket, or (B) pop out to the three-point area (Diagram 9-16).

(A) The Roll to the Basket

In Diagram 9-16, (4) screens for (1) and rolls to the ballside lay-up area that was vacated by (2). If (1) cannot pass to (4) on the roll or subsequent post up, (2) loops around (3) and (5) to the three-point area at the point.

After (1) passes to (2), (2) can shoot for three or reverse the ball to (3), coming out of (5)'s downscreen to the wing. See Diagram 9-17.

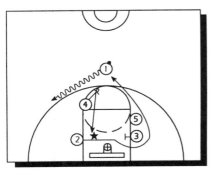

Diagram 9-16

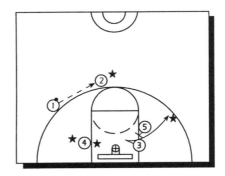

Diagram 9-17

The team is now in position to run a play from its basic 1-2-2 set. Shuffle teams often refer to this as a pattern set.

(B) The Pop to the Point

This time, after (4) screens for (1)'s dribble to the wing, (4) sees that X4, the defender, is hedging out to force (1) wide and allow X1 to get through. This tells (4) to fake the roll to the basket and pop to the point for a possible three-point shot. See Diagram 9-18.

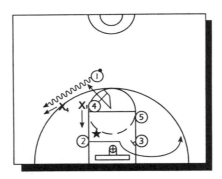

Pop to Point
Diagram 9-18

When (1) passes to (4) at the point and a shot is not forthcoming, (2) loops over (5), and continues to the low-post area. See Diagram 9-19.

(5) then screens down for (3), who pops to the wing. (4) passes to (3), who may shoot, and then (4) initiates a 1-2-2 set play via his or her cut. See Diagram 9-20.

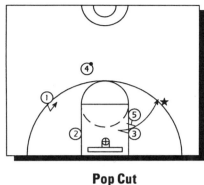

Loop Back
Diagram 9-19

Pop Cut
Diagram 9-20

VI. The Double Stack Lob Play

Diagram 9-21 shows (1) making dribble entry followed by (4)'s downscreen for (2).

After (1) passes to (2), screens down for (4), and (5) screens down for (3). (4) and (3) cut to their respective wings. See Diagram 9-22.

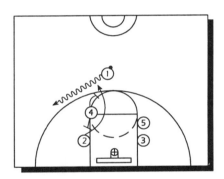

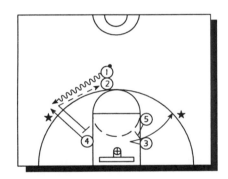

Double Stack Popout
Diagram 9-22

Diagram 9-21

(2) can shoot, or pass to either wing. In Diagram 9-23 (2) passes to (3) and this tells the offside post (1) to move up and screen for (2), who cuts to the basket looking for a possible lob pass from (3). (5) becomes the second option as (5) posts up with no offside defensive help.

If a shot does not develop from this action, (3) passes to (1), who screened and popped to the point. If X1 hedged on (2)'s cut, (1) may have the time and space to take a three pointer. If (1) cannot get a shot, (1) can initiate a basic 1-2-2 sequence.

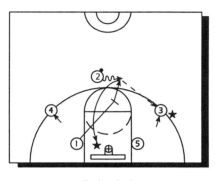

Point Lob
Diagram 9-23

Pressure Reliever

Wing Pick-Up Play

Once (1) makes the entry and picks up the dribble, many teams will pressure and attempt to deny a pass to teammates. To counter this ploy, (1) is taught to maintain the dribble as long as possible. The ballside post ((3) in Diagram 9-24) can cut to the corner and work a give and go play with (1). Point player (2) will make a change of direction and replace (1) at the wing.

If (1) is not open, (1) loops around (4) and (5) to the point. The ball is then reversed to (1) via (2). See Diagram 9-25.

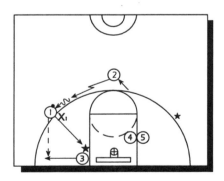

Diagram 9-24

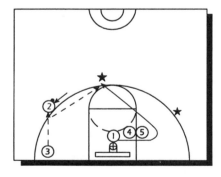

Diagram 9-25

This pressure-relieving option works well with all six dribble-entry box plays because once (1) dribbles to the wing, they all have a ballside post to cut to the corner, a point player to replace (1), and players in the lane for (1) to loop around.

Once a coach has chosen the dribble-entry box plays that best fit his or her personnel, the others may be held in reserve as secondary plays. These plays may then be added or replace the ones in use when and if needed.

Zone Potential

The dribble-entry box formation may be used against zones via the three pattern sets it can provide. These sets are the 1-2-2, the overload, and a wide 2-3 when three pointers are needed. In the following diagrams, player (2) is the person who keys the play options. (2) will determine the formation by the cut executed as (1) makes the dribble entry.

The 1-2-2 Formation

Diagram 9-26 shows (1) dribbling to the wing. (2), the ballside low-post player, starts across the lane and then hesitates as (3) cuts to the point off the downscreens of (4) and (5).

(2) then cuts under (4) and (5) and to the far wing position. (4) and (5) screen the zone for (2) and then (5) slices over (4) to the ballside post area. See Diagram 9-27.

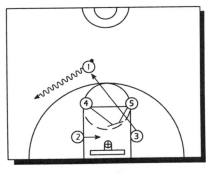

Key Goes Away
Diagram 9-26

Diagram 9-27

(1) can pass to (3) in order to reverse the ball to (2), or pass to (5) in the lane. See Diagram 9-28. (4) will screen, step up, post up on the popout option.

This puts the team in a 1-2-2 zone set.

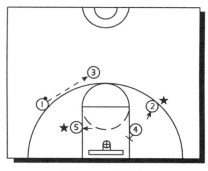

Diagram 9-28

The Overload

This time when (1) makes the dribble entry, (2) moves to the ballside corner or short corner and (3) cuts off (4) and (5) to the point. See Diagram 9-29.

(5) then slices over (4) to the ballside post and an overload is formed. The ball is passed around the overload triangles until a shot opens up. See Diagram 9-30.

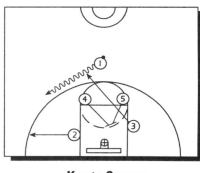

Key to Corner
Diagram 9-29

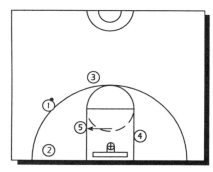

Overload
Diagram 9-30

Converting to a Wide 2-3 Three-Point Set

As (1) makes the dribble entry, (2) cuts off (4) to the ballside guard position. This cut tells (3) to move to the offside guard area using (5) as a screen. See Diagram 9-31.

(4) and (5) then cross as (4) cuts to the wide offside forward area, and (5) moves to the ballside post. See Diagram 9-32.

This set is an ideal one from which to obtain three-point opportunities. It also works well versus odd front (1-2-2 and 1-3-1) zones.

Having these three zone offensive formations available from the box and one dribble-entry play allows a team to present many varied challenges to a zone defense.

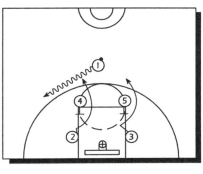

Key to High
Diagram 9-31

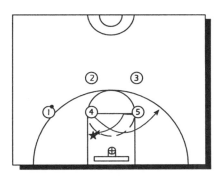

Two-Guard Front
Diagram 9-32

The preceding plan may be used by an up-tempo team throughout a game, or by an average-tempo team when time and score demand it.

Following is a method of using this offense as a "closer" when you are protecting a lead.

The Double Stack Control Game to the Box and One Dribble-Entry Closer

The Double Stack Control Game

The double stack offense is a dribbling game that allows a team to take control of a game in critical situations. It requires a specific type of personnel. You need at least one talented dribbler and two adequate ones. The three outside players in this stall must also be expert at keep-away and have better than average free throw-shooting skill. The two inside players can be defensive specialists of adequate size.

Diagram 9-33 shows (1) (the talented dribbler) bringing the ball into the front court and controlling it. (2) and (3) are stacked inside their big players (4) and (5), one step outside the lane with the top stacker at least as high as the lane.

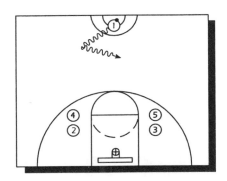

Diagram 9-33

(1), (2), and (3) must know the time and penetration rules, and the meaning of the term "closely guarded."

When (1) picks up the dribble after controlling the ball, the inside stacker on that side must use the post to pop to an open spot. If (1) is out in front, the stacker ((2) in Diagram 9-34) pops to the wing. If (1) has been forced to the side, (2) pops out front. See Diagram 9-35.

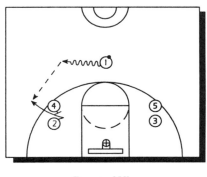

Pop to Wing
Diagram 9-34

Pop to Front
Diagram 9-35

As soon as the pass is made to the stacker (2), (1) replaces him or her and (2) controls the ball by dribbling. See Diagrams 9-36 and 9-37.

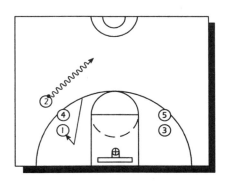

Diagram 9-36

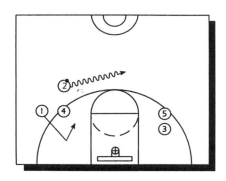

Diagram 9-37

Pressure Relief of Wing Denial
When an inside stacker ((2) in Diagram 9-38) steps out and is denied the pass by the defender, the offside small player (3) uses a big player to cut to the front.

If (3) is open, (1) passes to and replaces (3) as (3) controls the ball. (2) resets the stack on the side. See Diagram 9-39.

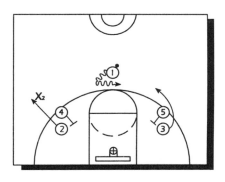

Diagram 9-38

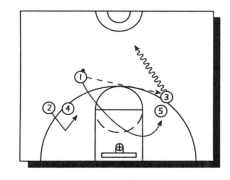

Pass and Reset
Diagram 9-39

If (3) is not open, (3) loops around (5) and cuts to the basket. Once in a while, (3) is open on this cut, but its real objective is to cause (5)'s defender to hedge by stepping into (3)'s path. This leaves (5) open who steps out front to receive the ball from (1). This all must happen quickly because (1) has picked up the dribble. See Diagram 9-40.

(1) then replaces (2), who comes to the point, receives the ball from (5), and attempts to control it. (5) returns to the stack. See Diagram 9-41.

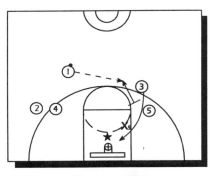

Diagram 9-40

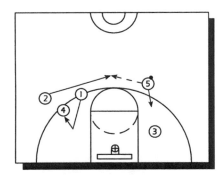

Diagram 9-41

The Scoring Play
This process is repeated until the shot clock reaches a desired time, usually six or seven seconds remaining in the possession or period. At this point, the dribbler with the ball (1) raises his or her (non-dribbling) hand. (1) then dribbles to a wing and a box and one dribble-entry play (i.e. double down) is run. See Diagrams 9-42 and 9-43.

Screen Away
Diagram 9-42

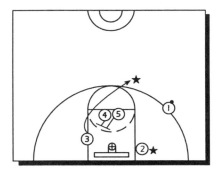

Double Down
Diagram 9-43

To use this clock-killing plan successfully, a coach must:

- have three adept keep-away players.
- design dribbling drills to sharpen their skills and give them confidence.
- review the time-penetration-closely guarded rules until the players are sure of them (hold-dribble-hold for maximum of four seconds each).
- devote much practice and game time to it before the key games begin.
- work out the proper transition time from the stall to the closer.

Not every coach will decide to have an up-tempo team. However, having a catch-up game when you are trailing and a clock-killing plan or control game to protect the lead when you are ahead are absolute necessities. If you can relate these two offensive tools by using the quick shot plays as "closers" for your time-killing motion, it will cut down on the precious practice time that is used to teach and hone them.

CHAPTER 10

The Wide Perimeter 2-3 Offense

This wide perimeter offensive set is an ultra-quick plan that flows directly from a team's three-point-oriented fast break. It may be used by an up-tempo team or by an average tempo team as a catch-up quick-shot alternative. In a clock-killing situation, it may be used as a closer following a control game by a team that has a talented post player and at least adequate outside shooters. Since this is a lot to expect, this chapter provides an alternate plan that features the high-post control game with a double-down quick-shot sequence as its "closer."

The Three-Point Fast Break

The basic half-court wide perimeter 2-3 offense may stem from a three-point fast break in which the players run directly to their three-point spots (see Diagram 10-1), or one in which they run through their outside lanes and back to their three-point areas (see Diagram 10-2).

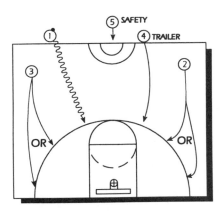

Trey Lanes
Diagram 10-1

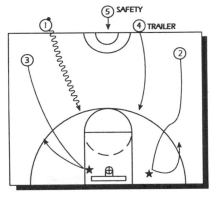

Basket and Out
Diagram 10-2

The Basic Half-Court Offense

The basic half-court offense can be run in two ways. If the team has a dominant post player, use the four-player motion with a single post. If you lack this strong post player, you should use the five-player motion.

Both of these plans encourage the three-point shot, stress proper spacing and ball movement, and have a three-point outside threat that complements its two-point inside options.

The Strong Post and Four Man Motion

To use this plan, your post (5) must be able to beat the defender one on one when the defender plays behind and have the skill and strength to attain position, catch a lob pass, and power up for two points when fronted. Since the post's teammates are located on the high-wide perimeter, (5) must also be an aggressive rebounder.

Diagram 10-3 shows the lead guard (1) picking up the dribble at the three-point line, and trailer (4) arriving at the line to complete the perimeter that includes (2) and (3) at the forward positions. (1) checks all the three-point options as pivot player (and fast break safety player) (5) sets up in the ballside post. (1) opts to pass to (4), who may shoot for three or pass to the forward (2), and initiate the motion. See Diagram 10-3.

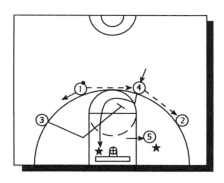

Lob Cut
Diagram 10-3

Post (5) comes to the new ballside and the offside forward arrives to set a screen on (4)'s defender.

(4) cuts off (3) to the offside lay-up area for a possible lob pass. This maneuver permits (5) to post up with little or no offside defensive help. (2) may lob to (4), pass directly in to (5) if the defender is behind, or lob if (5) is being fronted and has attained an advantageous position. If none of these immediate options is open, (2) may then pass to (3), who screened for (4) and popped to the three-point perimeter. (3) has a strong chance of being open if X3 hedged out and helped X4 get over the screen. See Diagram 10-4.

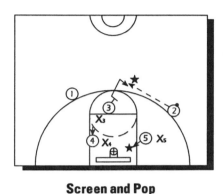

Screen and Pop
Diagram 10-4

If (3) has no shot, (3) looks inside to (5), or to (4), who looped around (1)'s downscreen. See Diagram 10-5. (4) can shoot or pass to (1) to repeat the motion. As always, (5) swings to the ballside. See Diagram 10-6.

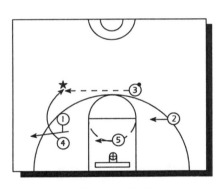

Diagram 10-5

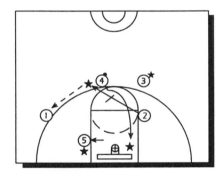

Diagram 10-6

The Skip Pass
During the strong low-post motion, the offside defender(s) will usually drop off and attempt to help in the lane. When this occurs, crosscourt skip passes may be thrown to the player he or she is guarding (X3 and (3)). See Diagram 10-7.

If nothing develops from this crosscourt pass, (3) may pass to (2), who screened and popped to the three-point area, or to (4) and restart the motion. See Diagram 10-8.

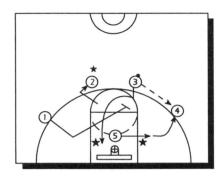

Skip Pass
Diagram 10-7

Lob Cut
Diagram 10-8

Coaching Point:
At least once in the first half of each game, the lob pass should be thrown. This will help establish an inside threat and loosen up the offside defenders. The net result will be more open three-point shots.

The Five-Player Wide Perimeter Motion

When you lack a dominant post player, the five-player motion may be run. This continuity is also run from a high-wide 2-3 set.

In Diagram 10-9 when guard (1) picks up the dribble, safety player (5) sets up in the *offside* post position. Then, when (1) passes to the forward (3), (1) cuts off a screen by (4) and slides to an open spot on the offside three-point perimeter. At the same time, (5) steps out to screen for (2), who cuts low to the ballside post area. (3) may shoot for three, pass to (1) for three, or pass inside to (2), for two points.

When a pass is made to (2), he or she usually shoots it. When the pass goes to (1), (1) may shoot, or pass to either (4) or (5), who both had screened and popped outside the three-point line. See Diagram 10-10.

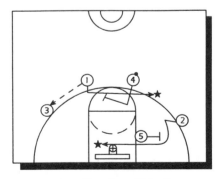

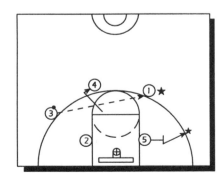

Baseline Shuffle—Side Screen
Diagram 10-9

Diagram 10-10

The ball is then moved around the perimeter until a pass is made from the weakside guard to the weakside forward. (See the pass from (1) to (5) in Diagram 10-11). This pass restarts the motion with (2) now acting as the offside post player. See Diagram 10-12.

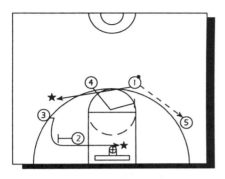

Shuffle Cut—Side Screen
Diagram 10-11

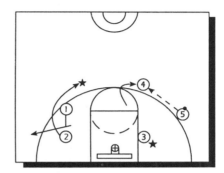

Diagram 10-12

The use of these two perimeter plans does not have to be an either or choice. A team could possibly use both of them in their offensive plan. The strong post four-player motion could be used when your post player can dominate the defender. When you are out-played in the post, the five player motion could be utilized. There may even be a game when match-ups would dictate that you use the strong post four-player motion, but with a forward who has a weak defender in the post and your big post (5) involved in the perimeter motion.

Pressure Reliever

The Roll or Pop Play

A simple method of relieving defensive pressure on the wide perimeter is the roll or pop play. Diagram 10-13 shows (1) with the ball and the other three perimeter players being overplayed and denied a pass. Seeing this, post (5) breaks to the high post and receives a bounce pass from (1). This tells both forwards ((2) and (3)) to screen for their respective guards. The guards, (1) and (4), slide to the three-point area at the free throw line extended.

(2) and (3) may then make an individual decision to either roll to the basket, or to pop to the three-point area. In Diagram 10-14, (3) chooses to roll and (2) opts to pop high.

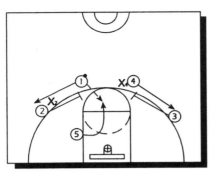

Screen Up-In
Diagram 10-13

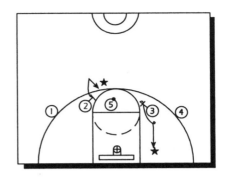

Pop or Roll
Diagram 10-14

(5) then passes to the open player as the players in the forward positions ((1) and (4)) balance the offense by replacing a roller (see (4) in Diagram 10-15), or staying at the forward position if the screener popped high. See (1) in Diagram 10-15.

After passing to the perimeter, (5) returns to the ballside low-post position and the basic motion is resumed. See Method I in Diagram 10-16.

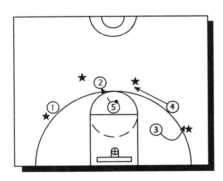

Diagram 10-15

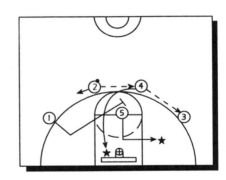

Lob Cut
Diagram 10-16

This quick hitter works well to relieve defensive pressure on the perimeter, and to provide variety to the offense.

A Secondary Play

Once a coach has chosen the three-point perimeter plan that best fits the personnel on hand, he or she may add the following play when and if needed.

The Perimeter Weave

This motion begins as (4), the trailer, arrives at the three-point line and receives the ball from (1). (4) dribbles toward the near corner and hands off to (3) in weave fashion. Seeing this key, (5) breaks to the high post (see Diagram 10-17) and (1) moves to exchange with (2).

(3) passes to (2) and cuts sharply inside of (2) uses (3)'s cut and (5)'s solid screen to penetrate the lane. See Diagram 10-18.

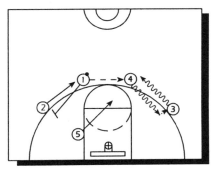

Diagram 10-17

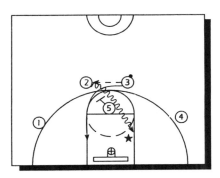

Diagram 10-18

When (2) is stopped, (2) looks to the perimeter for (5), who screened and popped high; (3), who looped around (1)'s downscreen; and (4), who cut to the baseline and back (made a V). See Diagram 10-19.

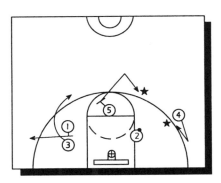

Diagram 10-19

Once the ball is passed back out to the perimeter and a shot is not forthcoming, the weave is restarted, and (2) (the penetrator) becomes the new high post. See Diagrams 10-20 and 10-21.

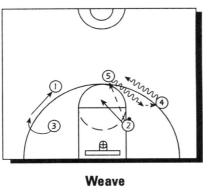
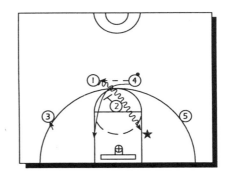

Weave
Diagram 10-20

Diagram 10-21

From there, the play is continued until a three-point shot, or an unmolested lay-up is acquired. This play works very well for teams that have strong dribblers, who can penetrate, and are talented outside shooters. Some defensive teams may trap a dribble weave, therefore caution is needed.

Zone Potential

These two wide perimeter player-to-player offensive plans use many of the techniques of zone offenses. They spread the defense via the wide and high perimeter, use skip passes and ball movement, in general, to get three-point shots, and attempt to penetrate with passes in and out of the pivot, plus dribbling. For example:

The Strong Post Perimeter Offense Versus Zones

Diagram 10-22 shows trailer (4) arriving to complete the wide and high four player perimeter and receiving a pass from lead guard (1). (4) then passes to (3) and cuts directly to the offside low post area without waiting for (2)'s screen. (2) hesitates and then cuts to the middle.

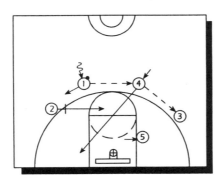

Diagram 10-22

The Triangle Play

(3) may pass to (2) in the middle of the zone, or pass crosscourt to (1) for a three-pointer. When (3) passes to (2), a zone triangle play results. (2) can square up and shoot it, or drop the ball inside to (4) or (5), for a power lay-up shot. See Diagram 10-23.

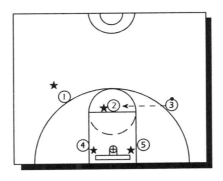

Triangle
Diagram 10-23

Ball Reversal

If (2) does not receive the pass from (3), (2) steps out to the ballside guard area. See Diagram 10-24.

Then, when (3) passes to (2), (1) screens down for (4), who cuts to the offside guard area and (2) reverses the ball to (4). See Diagram 10-25.

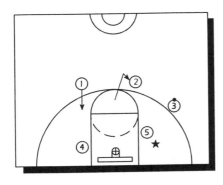

Diagram 10-24

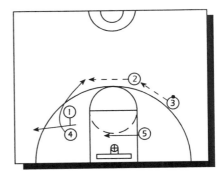

Reverse
Diagram 10-25

Start Over

From there, the process is repeated. This simple play allows a team to alternate the offensive perimeter from even to odd to even. It also tests the zone's middle with a triangle play and has a planned skip pass leading to a three-point shot. All these options are within the context of a wide perimeter that elongates the zone slides and makes them more difficult to execute.

The Clock-Killing Phase

So far, this chapter has covered ideas that are designed for an up-tempo team, or an average team attempting to play "catch-up." The third phase of this basketball offense allows a team to run the shot clock down to a desired time and then obtain a high-percentage shot. This team technique has become a necessity because leads that were fairly safe in the past can now disappear in a flurry of three-pointers by your opponent. It can best be accomplished by running one of the proven control games that operate from the same pattern set as your basic offense until the proper time on the shot clock arrives and then using the "quick hitter" portion of your offensive plan as a "closer." This chapter uses the high-post stall as the time killer and the strong low-post wide perimeter play as the "closer." Then, since this plan requires such a specifically skilled type of personnel, a second method is provided. It, too, uses the high-post control game as the time killer, but it closes with a double-down quick-shot series that works better for teams with more average personnel.

The High-Post Control Game to the Strong Low-Post Closer

One of the best and most widely used control games is the high-post one. It is run from a 2-1-2 set and consists of three basic plays. They are keyed by passes made from the guard position, which are the (A) guard-to-guard pass, (B) guard-to-forward pass, and (C) the guard-to-post pass.

(A) The Guard-to-Guard Pass
A guard-to-guard pass keys a single offside exchange. See Diagram 10-26.

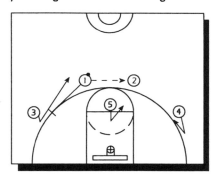

Diagram 10-26

(B) The Guard-to-Post Pass

A guard-to-post pass keys a double guard-forward exchange. See Diagram 10-27.

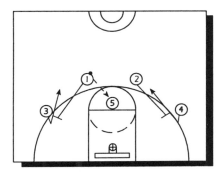

Diagram 10-27

(C) The Guard-to-Forward Pass

The third play is used to loosen up the defense by presenting a scoring threat. In Diagram 10-28, (1) passes to (3) and clears out by cutting down the lane and quickly to the far side. The offside guard (2) makes a jab step toward the ball and slashes off high post (5) to the ballside lay-up area. (5) is instructed to step out and set a definite screen, much like the "headhunter" screen used by passing game teams. (5) should be certain to give X2 sufficient distance and time to make the screen legal (never more than two steps). See Diagram 10-28.

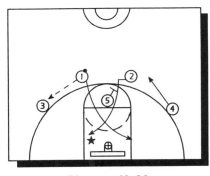

Diagram 10-28

If (2) does not get open for a shot, (3) dribbles out front and (4) replaces (2). (1) and (2) become the forwards.

High-Post Control Game Pressure Relievers

The teasing effect of the high-post control game motion causes most teams to give up on their pressure and help rules and resort to one-on-one overplay denial with little offside help. This opens up the possibility of many backdoor situations. They must be pointed out to your team and drilled on, until they become second nature. Here are some of them:

Post Backdoor

Post (5) will eventually be overplayed and you can direct lob to him or her from the guard or forward position. See Diagram 10-29.

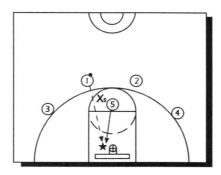

Diagram 10-29

Wing Backdoor

On a guard-to-post pass, the onside forward, who has been denied a pass from the defender, can backdoor. Both passes (1) to (5) and (5) to (3) should be bounce passes. See Diagram 10-30.

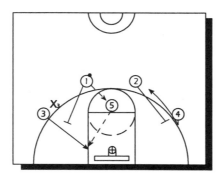

Diagram 10-30

Delayed Wing Backdoor

On a guard-to-forward pass, the guard who cleared out can run a direct backdoor cut once the forward with the ball dribbles out front and passes to the opposite forward, who came out front. See Diagrams 10-31 and 10-32.

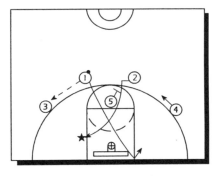

Diagram 10-31

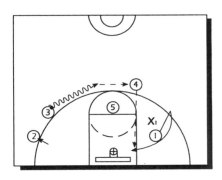

Diagram 10-32

The Strong Low-Post "Closer"

The high-post control game is run to a predetermined time on the shot clock. At that moment, a guard ((1) in Diagram 10-33) passes to forward (3) and post (5), keys the transition to the "closer" phase by cutting to the ballside post area. If (5) is open, (3) passes to him or her at an angle that keeps the advantageous position on the defender. If (5) is being fronted and denied the pass, the offside forward (2) cuts down and then up to the free throw line to receive a pass from (3). Upon receiving this pass, (2) looks inside for (5), who has assumed a wide stance in an attempt to trap X5 in a poor defensive position to prevent him or her powering to the basket. See Diagram 10-34.

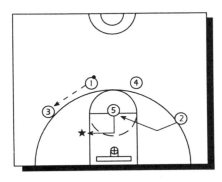

Diagram 10-33

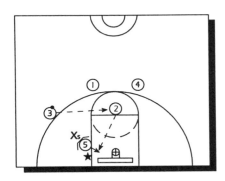

Diagram 10-34

When (1) sees that (3) cannot pass to (5) or (2), (1) cuts to the offside lay-up area using (2) as a natural screen. See Diagram 10-35.

If (3) cannot lob to (1), (3) may pass to (2), who screened and popped to the three-point area, or skip pass to (4) on the offside three-point perimeter. (4) may be open if the defender dropped off to help in the lane. See Diagram 10-36.

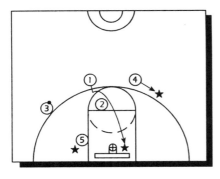

Diagram 10-35

Diagram 10-36

In most cases, when (5) is not open, (3) passes to (2) and (4) screens down for (1). If (1) does not have a shot, (1) reverses the ball to (4) and the play is repeated. See Diagram 10-37.

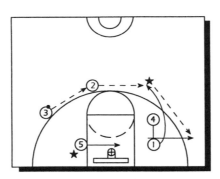

Diagram 10-37

Teams that lack the specialized personnel to run this "closer" may use the double-down series.

The Double-Popout Quick-Shot Series as the "Closer"

Once the clock has been run down via the high-post control game, one of the guards ((1) in Diagrams 10-38) keys the transition to the double-down series by raising a non-dribbling arm and calling out "double." (1) then passes to (3), the forward on the ballside and (1) and (2) make the same cuts they made after a guard-to-forward pass when running the high-post control game. This time, however, they post-up low.

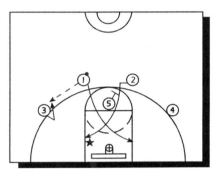

Diagram 10-38

(5) may then key either of two plays. (5) may step out to the point and call the basic double-popout play, or screen for (3) to initiate the screen and roll to double down play.

The Basic Double-Popout Play
Diagram 10-39 shows (5) stepping to the point and receiving a pass from (3). (3) and (4) then screen down for the guard in their low-post area.

(5) may pass to either wing or directly inside to (3) or (4). In Diagram 10-40, (5) chooses to pass to wing (1). After passing to a wing, (5) always screens away for the offside post player as for (3) in this example.

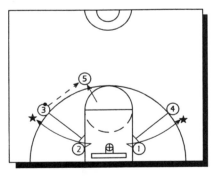
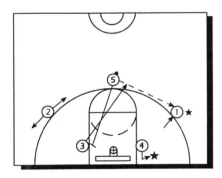

Diagram 10-39   **Diagram 10-40**

In this short time situation, (1)'s first option is to get the ball inside to (4). (1) may also: shoot it, pass crosscourt to (2) whose defender may be helping in the lane, or to (3) moving to the point off (5)'s downscreen. If (4) is being fronted, (3) may also use a lob. This option is possible because (5)'s screen for (3) engages the primary offside help. See Diagram 10-41.

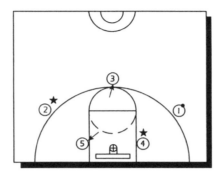

Diagram 10-41

When (1) passes to (3) at the point, (3) looks first to (4) inside for a change of angles pass. If (4) is not open inside, (1) and (2) screen down for (4) and (5), and the basic play is repeated. See Diagram 10-42. This time, (3) passes to (4) at the wing and screens away for the offside post (2). See Diagram 10-43.

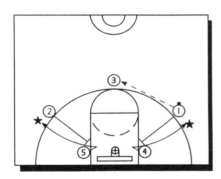

Diagram 10-42

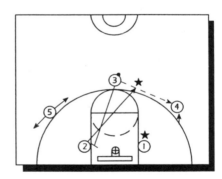

Diagram 10-43

Coaching Point

This basic pattern may be tailored to fit a specific team. If you have a player you want to be in the post-up area as much as possible or a downscreener who is a weak post player, you can have the wing fake the downscreen (see Diagram 10-44) or loop around the post player (see Diagram 10-45).

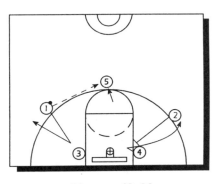

Diagram 10-44

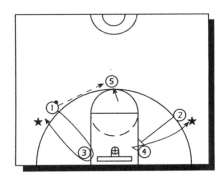

Diagram 10-45

Another good move may be used when (5) is guarded by a dominant big defender.

After the initial cuts by (1) and (2), when the ball has been passed to (5) at the point, this variation may be used. Instead of (5) passing to a wing and screening down for the offside post, he or she will wait and receive the screen and cut to the offside lay-up area for a possible lob pass. In Diagram 10-46, (5) passes to (2) and receives the screen from (4). Big defender X5 is guarding (5) and (4) is instructed to force a switch that would keep (5) away from the rebound area. If this cannot be accomplished, (4) must at least make it very difficult for X5 to get through. Also, if X5 is too aggressive, (4) may be able to draw a step-in foul on X5.

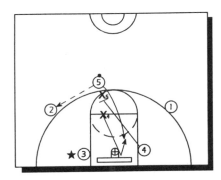

Diagram 10-46

Then, if (2) can get the ball into (3), who should be a strong post player, the chances of getting a high-percentage shot and, when needed, a second shot, are improved.

The Screen and Roll to Double Popout Play
In Diagram 10-47 (1) passes to (3) and (1) and (2) again make their cuts to their low-post areas.

This time, however, (5) chooses to call the screen and roll play. (5) does this by stepping out to screen for (3). See Diagram 10-48.

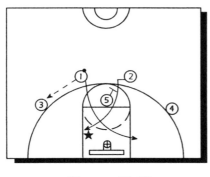

Diagram 10-47

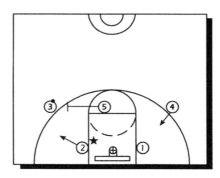

Diagram 10-48

(3) uses (5)'s screen by dribbling off it and into the lane. This screen tells (2) to clear the lane by cutting to the wing. After screening, (5) rolls to the basket and then (4) screens down for (1), who pops to the wing. See Diagram 10-49.

(3) may shoot, hit the roller (5), or pass to either wing, and start the basic motion. In Diagram 10-50, (3) starts the motion by passing to (1) and screening for the offside post (5).

Screen and Roll
Diagram 10-49

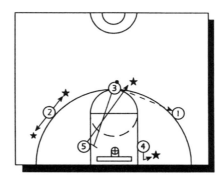

Diagram 10-50

Combining this double-popout series with the high-post stall allows a team to kill the clock and still end up with a high-percentage shot. The scoring options that are included make it a viable plan for an average team.

THE AUTHORS

As the basketball coach at Eastern Montana College (now Montana State University-Billings) for sixteen seasons, Coach Harkins' teams won 295 games, ten NAIA district titles, and twelve conference championships. He also coached four teams in international competition.

Coach Harkins also served as Professor of Health, Physical Education and Recreation at Eastern Montana College, where he received the college's award for outstanding achievement in scholarship and creativity. In addition, he was awarded Akron University's Distinguished Alumni Award.

Jerry Krause has coached basketball at elementary, secondary, college and Olympic developmental levels for over 34 years. He served for 30 years as research chairman for the National Association of Basketball Coaches. Krause has served as President of the NAIA Basketball Coaches Association and also on the Board of Directors of the NABC. He has served the longest tenure (15 years) of anyone on the NCAA Basketball Rules Committee where he was also chairman. He is most respected for his emphasis (books and videos) on the fundamental skills of basketball. Krause is presently Professor of Sport Philosophy at the United States Military Academy in West Point, New York.

ADDITIONAL BASKETBALL RESOURCES FROM

■ **_THREE-POINT FIELD GOAL OFFENSE_**
FOR MEN AND WOMEN'S BASKETBALL
by Harry L. "Mike" Harkins and Jerry Krause
1997 ▪Paper▪ 112 pp
ISBN 1-57167-138-2 ▪ $15.00 each

■ **_ZONE OFFENSES_**
FOR MEN AND WOMEN'S BASKETBALL
by Harry L. "Mike" Harkins and Jerry Krause
1997 ▪Paper▪ 132 pp
ISBN 1-57167-139-0 ▪ $15.00

■ **_MOTION GAME OFFENSES_**
FOR MEN AND WOMEN'S BASKETBALL
by Harry L. "Mike" Harkins and Jerry Krause
1997 ▪Paper▪ 145 pp
ISBN 1-57167-136-6 ▪ $15.00

■ **_ATTACKING ZONE DEFENSES (2ND ED)_**
by John Kresse and Richard Jablonski
1997 ▪Paper▪ 128 pp
ISBN 1-57167-047-5 ▪ $15.00

TO PLACE YOUR ORDER:
U.S. customers call
TOLL FREE (800)327-5557,
or write
COACHES CHOICE Books, P.O. Box 647, Champaign, IL 61824-0647,
or FAX: (217) 359-5975